If Love Hurts

J Davey

If Love Hurts

Copyright © 2016 J Davey

ISBN: 978-0-9955471-0-0

First published in the United Kingdom in 2016
by Faith, Hope and Love Publishing.

PRAISE FOR *IF LOVE HURTS*

"You have given me the courage to get help and try to move on. Very informative. A great read."
Megan

"Powerful from the start, had me engaged and wanting to keep reading from the very first page. This book will help others in similar situations know they have the power and strength to leave."
Jane

"Brilliantly written information about being in a domestic abuse relationship. I wished I had this information before I entered a relationship with what I soon found out to be a mentally and emotionally abusive partner."
Sandra

"Both informative and inspirational, this book, written from J Davey's personal perspective, will give hope and strength to those in similar situations."
Lee

"Great read with very real life situations. Made me pick up it up again and read."
Casey-Leigh

CONTENTS

Foreword   1
Preface   3

SECTION 1

My Story

Chapter 1   How Love Hurt Me   7
Chapter 2   When Hurt Is Abuse   26

SECTION 2

Tactics They Use

Chapter 3   Using His Body   30
Chapter 4   Using His Words   33
Chapter 5   Using Your Emotions   39
Chapter 6   Using Money   49

SECTION 3

Why Do They Do It?

Chapter 7   Their Past   54
Chapter 8   Alcohol   57
Chapter 9   Mental Illness   61

SECTION 4

Effects Of An Abusive Relationship

Chapter 10   Effects On The Partner   68
Chapter 11   Effects On The Children   79

SECTION 5

Change in Abusive Relationships

Chapter 12   Will He Ever Change?   86

SECTION 6

Christian Relationships

Chapter 13   Abuse in Christian Relationships   91

SECTION 7

Loving Life Again

Chapter 14   To Leave or Stay   103
Chapter 15   Leaving Safely   106
Chapter 16   Finances   113
Chapter 17   Healing the Hurt   122
Chapter 18   Loving Life   132

Note from the Author   137
About the Author   138

Further Help   139

FOREWORD

I love this book and am recommending it to all survivors- it is essential reading, it's brutally truthful, articulated beautifully and with highly accurate to life harrowing ordeals.

The constant tension of being attached to a partner who has NPD is almost like a magnet for an empathic person - you want to help, it's confusing, and 'crazy making' from one of the vilest villains (the DV perpetrator) and he's in many homes abusing others.

Each chapter, I'm drawn in further to this web. It's so very real of the accounts I hear from the emotional abuse, the physical entitlement to the carefully dismantled Nazi depleting of a woman's Self.

You are not alone is the message, survivors need to stand together and read this. What used to be Britain's best kept secret now has had the doors blown off.

J Davey's genius shines like a beacon and helps shed light from an insiders point on what is possibly the scariest attacker ever- one from inside your own home

David Kilmurry (Dip Hyp Mbicch)

(Cognitive Behavioural Hypnotherapist - he is well known for his rehabilitation treatments for survivors of Domestic Violence)

www.davidkilmurry.com

PREFACE

'Love hurts,
Love scars,
Love wounds and marks
Any heart not tough or strong enough
To take a lot of pain, take a lot of pain
Love is like a cloud, it holds a lot of rain
Love hurts,
Ooo-oo love hurts'

(Nazareth: Love Hurts)

From songs to television shows and books, it seems widely accepted that love hurts at times. To an extent it is probably true.

A child may be upset by the parent saying that they can't have the latest game console or not allowing them to be out as late as their friends.

A husband may feel rejected because his wife says that she is too tired to have sex.

A wife may feel angry towards her husband because he is watching a football match on the television and not responding to her.

3

We all hurt others even though we don't do so intentionally.

The parent doesn't want her child to be upset but knows that it is not in the child's best interest to get whatever they demand. It may be better to wait until their birthday to give them the game console they desperately want and it may not be safe for the child to be travelling home late at night.

The wife may be too tired to have sex because she has been up every night feeding a small baby. She is not saying she is too tired in order to hurt her husband, but feels that she doesn't have the energy at that time.

The husband may simply be so engrossed in the football match that he doesn't hear his wife speak to him. He is not ignoring her to make her angry - he simply hasn't heard her.

As shown in these examples, when we are in a relationship, we may unintentionally hurt someone or someone may hurt us.

The key word is *unintentionally*. When it is unintentional, we will strive to resolve the conflict and mend the hurt that we may have caused. That doesn't mean that the child gets whatever they want, the wife is no longer tired or the husband should stop watching football on the television. What it means is that we try to recognise each other's feelings, are able to express our opinions and reach an agreement, compromise or understanding.

This is how we love each other - through compassion, empathy, being supportive and understanding. Placing someone else's needs above our own and ensuring that they feel cared for.

However, in some relationships this doesn't happen. In some relationships, love hurts too often. In some relationships, hurt is intentional.

Some relationships are abusive.

But it can be difficult to distinguish between unintentional hurt and abusive hurt, which is why those in abusive relationships are often confused, full of inner conflict and may feel as though they are going mad.

How do I know this? Because I was in an abusive relationship for almost 20 years.

I felt the confusion of not being able to work out what was wrong in my marriage, yet knowing that something was. The confusion of not knowing if what I was experiencing was a normal part of marriage or not. The confusion of not being able to understand the rollercoaster of emotions that I felt every day.

The inner conflict of believing that marriage was important and not to be thrown away, yet being constantly exhausted at trying ways to fix the relationship. The conflict of wanting to create a secure two-parent family unit for my children, but without them being affected by the tension in the house. The conflict of wanting to help my husband with his own hurt while also wanting him to stop hurting me.

I felt that I was going mad. Each time that I thought I understood what was bothering him and how he felt, something changed again. The words that he said in one conversation would contradict with his words in a later conversation. Nothing matched up or made sense, leaving me to think that I was going crazy.

I've written this book because I struggled with confusion and inner conflict during my marriage. I've written this book to show you that you're not going mad if love is hurting, nothing you have tried is working and nothing makes sense.

During my marriage, I thought that I was the only one experiencing those emotions which resulted in me not sharing my feelings with my friends and family. However, I now know, from talking to others, that my experiences and hurt are sadly experienced by others - both men and women - in relationships, yet they often feel alone as I did.

So, in this book, I am going to openly share the story of my marriage with you (a lot of which I haven't told anyone else), explore the hidden secrets of domestic abuse and discuss how to love life again.

While statistically, men are more likely to be the abuser in a physically abusive relationship, both men and women can be and are abusive to their partners. However, for the simplicity of pronouns in this book, I will identify the abuser as male and the victim as female.

SECTION 1 – MY STORY

1
HOW LOVE HURT ME

I'm not a professional counsellor, I've not written a dissertation on domestic abuse and I've not worked in the field of marriage therapy. However, I was in a negative and abusive relationship for almost 20 years and I've decided to openly share my story to show how complex an abusive relationship is and how the choices that are made are not straightforward. As we were together for such a long time, I will keep to the main aspects of our relationship and will retell the past events as I viewed them at the time so that you can understand my perspective.

Later in this book, when exploring specific behaviours of domestic abuse and the impact of these, I will describe particular aspects of my relationship to illustrate the tactics that are used.

The Love of my Life

My mum says that from a young age I was stubborn and independent, so it probably wasn't a huge surprise that a week after my 16th birthday I left home to move in with family friends who lived 200 miles away from my family. While I lived there I studied three A-levels at college and worked part-time in a shop, enjoying meeting new people and having some freedom.

Almost exactly a year later, and just after my 17th birthday, I met the person who I thought was the love of my life (who I will call Mark) at a mutual friend's party. He was older than me by five years and was separated from his wife at the time. We spent the whole evening talking and it was amazing. We just seemed to click.

I felt able to open up to him about my problems and he was so understanding and supportive. In turn, he opened up to me about his past experiences. His brother and mother had physically abused him, leaving him with deep unresolved hurts. If that wasn't enough, his estranged wife had had an affair with his best friend and left him. Mark had lost his home, was in debt and had not a penny to his name due to his wife taking everything and the cost of the divorce. He appeared vulnerable and honest, which drew me towards him as I just wanted to take the hurt away.

His wife and I never came into contact but I saw the hurt that she had caused, especially when she accused him in the divorce paperwork of having an alcohol problem, spending all the money out of their joint account and even physically assaulting her. She sounded evil and malicious. As he had supported me with my problems, I supported him when he was feeling angry and hurt because of her allegations. After all, that was what being in a relationship was all about - sharing problems and supporting each other.

For Richer or Poorer

It seemed only natural to move into the shared house he lived in a few months later. We had no money - I was still doing my A-levels and he was working as a care assistant in a nursing home. But that didn't matter because I was so in love with him. In a way the lack of money almost seemed romantic - staying in love despite it all.
To try and help the situation I got a job as commis chef in the evenings, so I could continue to be at college in the day. Despite

both of us working, we still never had any money and struggled to find enough money to buy food.

What I didn't have in material goods, Mark made sure I had in compliments and gestures. He would continually tell me that I was attractive and looked great in everything that I wore. When I was upset or stressed, he would always provide a listening ear and give me a cuddle. Mark cared about me deeply and I couldn't believe that I had met someone so perfect.

One day, I came home from college and went to our money pot so that I could take £2 out for a Student Card that I needed for student identification in order to take my final A-level exams. The money pot was empty. When Mark staggered into the room, it was clear why. He had been in the pub on his day off and drunk our money away. It caused our first argument.

Mark admitted that he shouldn't have done it and apologised continually, explaining that he had gone to the pub because he was so bored and lonely while I was at college. He had missed me so much that it had led to him drink the day away. It was hard to be hurt when he clearly loved me so much that he didn't want to be apart from me. We managed to borrow the money from a friend so no harm was done and our first argument was forgotten.

I did quite well on my A-levels and went to university to study a law degree. However, during the first term break, I found out that I was pregnant.

It was quite a shock, but we both wanted children in a secure family, so we decided that I should leave university and get married immediately. It just felt like the right thing to do despite the speed. Within weeks, at the age of 18, I was married at the registry office and looking forward to the future.

Mark was ecstatic at the prospect of being a dad and shared with me his hurt when he found out that his ex-wife had aborted two of his children behind his back. Despite not being planned, this baby was the best thing to happen to both of us - to heal his hurts and have a family of our own.

My pregnancy seemed to bring us closer and Mark stopped going to the pub. Instead he drank at home, saying that he wanted to be with me and the baby rather than at the pub. I was touched by how much he cared as I knew that so many other partners would have been drinking out with their friends and coming home drunk. I felt lucky and special.

Fraying Tempers and Family Times

Just a year after our first baby was born we had bought a house, were both working hard and planning a second baby. We had some arguments but who doesn't? And it wasn't as though Mark wouldn't apologise afterwards, because he always did. Most of the time there were no reasons for the arguments. Mark would just seem stressed and angry which would lead to him shouting, slamming doors and pacing the room.

I couldn't blame him for getting angry at times. It was due to stress at work, his anger towards his family and ex-wife, or the pressure of renovating a house with little funds. He didn't mean to take it out on me when he was in a bad mood; it was just because I was the only one there at the time and he was under a lot of pressure.

Our second baby was born two years after our first. I simply loved being a mum. It was hard work and tiring but I loved it. Mark enjoyed being a dad too and loved nothing more than coming home from work and having a cuddle with his babies. Those times as a family of four were filled with happiness.

Exactly two years later I found out that I was unexpectedly pregnant with another baby and I worried that I would never manage with an extra one. I was already shattered trying to juggle the demands of a house, children and work. Of course Mark was working too, and as he worked more hours in his job compared to my two part-time jobs, it was clear that it was my responsibility to keep the house clean and tidy. There were no arguments or big discussions about our roles - Mark refused to do any housework and expected me to do it as I worked less hours. I'll admit to sometimes feeling resentment at having to do everything in the home, but I also understood that as I worked less, it was fair for me to do more hours on the housework.

Money Issues

When the children were in bed we were having more arguments. They were often about money. Mark's credit cards were over £8,000 in debt, although what he spent on the cards was never clear. He said it was food, nappies and decorating the house but, despite me asking, he refused to show me the bills.

Fortunately, Mark had the idea of consolidating his debts into a secured loan on the house which would reduce both the monthly payments and financial pressure. I was very nervous of taking on that much debt, because it would be in joint names and it was more than my annual salary at the time, but there seemed no other options as we simply couldn't afford Mark's monthly credit card payments.

Whether it was the stress of having three small children, worrying about finances or the continuation of Mark's bad moods and resulting arguments, I felt that I needed to do something for me. Starting my studies again by studying for an Open University degree seemed a good option and I hoped it would lead to a better job in the long-term.

When I told Mark my plans he wasn't happy about it. He refused to talk to me all night, leaving me trying to work out why he was upset. It wasn't the first time that he had done this. Instead of yelling and getting angry, he would sometimes go to the bedroom and refuse to speak to me without any explanation. It was more confusing than the shouting because I had no idea what I had done to make him ignore me and would lie awake worrying about what was wrong. I hated the tension in the air - it felt suffocating and produced a knot in my stomach.

The next day he was a different person, telling me that he would fully support me even though we couldn't afford it. Knowing that he was right and we couldn't afford the £50 a month with the debt that we had, I took on another job to pay for it. It stopped the comments that were making me feel guilty about spending money on myself.

Anger and Confusion

Over the next couple of years Mark's drinking increased and he moved from just shouting and slamming doors, to smashing things up and throwing things around when the little ones were in bed. Sometimes, when he did this, I would try and leave the room but he would stop me by standing in the doorway and puffing out his chest, or he would pin me against the wall by placing his hands either side of my body and his bulk in front of me. He said that it was acceptable as he had never laid a finger on me and he would never hit me, unlike some men out there. He always emphasised that he was better than others because he wasn't (in his words) a 'wife-beater'.

When he was shouting and being physically aggressive, I learnt that he couldn't be reasoned with. It felt as though he was not in control of himself. So I either stayed quiet to melt into the background or hid away when he was at his worst.

It probably seems obvious that our relationship was not healthy and maybe that I should have left at this point. Leaving was a constant conflict in my mind at this time. On the one hand there was an angry husband who made me feel confused and hurt, but on the other hand there was a loving and supportive husband who just needed some help and support to defeat the angry demons. Also, when sober and apologetic, Mark would tell me that he only did it because of what he had suffered as a kid - things that were so awful he couldn't bring himself to tell me the details. I reasoned that as it wasn't his fault, I should keep to my marriage vows to be there 'for better or for worse' and support Mark to be a better husband.

In addition, he always apologised and bought me flowers or

chocolates, so I believed that he was genuinely sorry for the shouting, smashing stuff up etc. If he was sorry then I should forgive him - a conviction that was also emphasised in Christian books and at Church.

Self Harm

Unfortunately, things turned worse when our then youngest was three years old. I returned from work in the early hours to find Mark still awake and ranting that the computer was broken and couldn't be fixed. As there were photos of the children and my university work was on the computer I became upset, but that just caused Mark to slam the lounge door and storm off to bed, leaving me to wonder why he was taking it out on me.

Waking the next morning I found myself alone in bed and instantly knew something was wrong as I was usually the first one up. The children were awake and asking for breakfast but I couldn't find Mark. In the kitchen I found a suicide note on the worktop and my heart simply stopped. Despite our relationship being difficult at times, I loved him and the thought of him leaving us in this way broke me in two. Getting through those hours, worrying about where he was or even whether he was dead or alive, was incredibly difficult. I didn't want the children to know anything was wrong so I tried to carry on as normal.

When the hospital phoned later that morning to say that he was safe I cried with relief. But then I was filled with anger. While he was being looked after by a team of doctors and nurses, I had been going mad with worry and he hadn't thought to ask them to phone me earlier, leaving me in a state of panic for hours.

Mark came home that afternoon with bandages on his wrists, to cover the cuts and stitches, and an apology. The range of emotions that I was feeling, from deep concern, to anxiety and confusion, to anger, were kept hidden. If Mark was suicidal and unable to cope with his own emotions, then I couldn't express my feelings and expect him to manage mine as well as his. I also couldn't turn to my friends and family for support as Mark told me that he couldn't cope with anyone else knowing. It became our secret.

For months afterwards I stayed awake at night until I was sure that he was asleep, so that I could make sure that he wasn't going to go off and do it again while I was sleeping. I was constantly anxious and felt that I couldn't leave his side.

The big question was why he had done it. In the lead up to that day nothing had changed between us, and the only thing that had happened was the computer breaking. He told me that he was sexually abused by a babysitter and he couldn't cope with the memories of childhood abuse any longer. There were so many traumas in his past, from the physical abuse from his mother and brother, to sexual abuse and then the treatment from his ex-wife, that I could understand he felt overwhelmed by it all. I encouraged him to see his doctor to be able to have counselling, but he refused saying that he only wanted to tell me his problems and nobody else. I didn't know what I could say or do to help him, but felt under pressure to make him better. I was beginning to feel overwhelmed with the responsibility of caring for him as well as the children and working. I felt low and unable to manage, but I couldn't see any other option but to manage.

The Rollercoaster

A year later we decided to move, saying that it would be a new start away from the bad memories. The debts would be cleared with the sale of the house. Mark was happy working for the police while I was happy in my job. We even went on a marriage course at our church to work on improving our relationship which resulted in me feeling closer to Mark and Mark being calmer.

Finally, I felt as though the past was behind us, that I was right to have fought for our marriage, and that we could have the relationship that we had when we first met. Things improved so much that I suggested having another baby. There would be a gap of nine years between this new baby and our third child but that wasn't a problem; I was excited to be able to have a baby in this 'new' relationship that I had with my husband. I was pregnant with our fourth baby within weeks of us deciding to try.

Sadly, the change in Mark's behaviour and our marriage didn't last long. During the pregnancy the drinking increased and the aggressive behaviour returned. Mark started to get drunk, shout and smash things up. When I got upset or angry, he would leave the house. I would then spend the next few hours worrying as he wouldn't answer my texts and if he did, they would hint that he was going to kill himself. As he had made a suicide attempt before, I was scared that he was serious when he made the threats and thought that if he did die, it would be my fault.

I would stay up until he returned home and I knew he was safe. Sometimes he wouldn't return to the house but go to his car and stay in there instead. I would only know that he was safe by going out several times over those hours he was missing and checking the car, hoping that he was in there. Every time he returned (either to the home or his car), he would be very drunk so there was no chance of discussing anything. It was better to leave him to sleep it off. The mornings always brought silence as he refused to talk about the night before, leaving constant questions in my mind as I tried to fit the pieces together but, invariably, I was left confused and anxious.

It took me quite a while to work out that he only did this on days when I was working in the morning and he wasn't. So I would be up until 4am – worrying, upset and hurt and then need to go to work at 7:30am, while he had a lie in and a day off. The exhaustion added to the confusion of trying to work out what was wrong, hence I spent a lot of time feeling as though I was in a fog, trying to make sense of something that had no logic.

He would deliberately start arguments over anything and nothing, twisting my words and contradicting himself, leaving me feeling as though I was going crazy as I tried to follow his points. My mind felt scrambled and unable to think, resulting in me questioning my own mind. I tried different tactics from ignoring him to shouting back, from trying to calm him to telling him that he was hurting me, but nothing seemed to make any difference.

Mark's explosive anger became part of our relationship and I couldn't make it go away. Accepting that Mark's anger was just part of our relationship seemed to minimise and normalise it. Also he wasn't angry all of the time and he hadn't physically hurt the children, so he could still be a good dad. He could still be loving and attentive - running me a hot bath when I came home from work, buying me some chocolate or supporting me when I was stressed at work. So, despite his outbursts, we decided to have one last baby.

Two Bombshells

Again, it didn't take long to conceive. When I was 7 months pregnant, he dropped two bombshells. Firstly, that he was being tested for bowel cancer and was worried sick that he had it. Secondly, that he had more than £20,000 of debt on different credit cards and he couldn't make the repayments any more.

I felt as though I had been kicked in the stomach and felt totally betrayed. I was torn about what to do. If he had cancer, then I should stand by him and care for him. If he didn't, then I was in two minds as to whether to leave him or not. He had deceived me by spending over £20,000 and he refused to produce a single credit card statement to show me what he had spent the money on. Yet, I had stuck with him through so much and I wanted a secure family unit to bring my children up in. I didn't want to give up on our marriage after so many years. It would have meant that everything that I had been through would have been for nothing.

I offered to go to our GP with him to get the results of the cancer tests in case it was bad news. However, he refused to let me go, saying that he had put me through enough and it wasn't fair to expect me to support him further.

After a tense week in which he barely spoke to me, Mark finally told me that the cancer test was clear and that he was so ashamed of what he had done to me and the children.

He seemed very genuine in his apology and I decided, for the sake of the children, and because I didn't want to give in after being together for so long, that I would stay with him. I was also scared to leave because I didn't know how to go about it, how I would manage alone or how he would react if I said I wanted to leave. So, instead of leaving, I stayed and helped him sort the financial mess.

While he was in an apologetic mood and promising to change I managed to persuade him to go to Alcoholics Anonymous to finally receive help for his drinking. If he would stop drinking, then I was sure that he would stop shouting and being aggressive. I was sure that he would go back to being the man that I met all those years ago and we could have a happy marriage again.

Mark agreed to go, but after two sessions he announced that he was cured and no longer needed any help. He didn't stop drinking but assured me that he was in control of it, rather than the drink being in control of him. I desperately wanted to believe this but knew deep down that nothing had changed. Someone who drinks alcohol every day isn't cured after two sessions.

At the same time, our third child, who was eleven years old, started having prolonged fainting spells, lasting up to an hour each, which resulted in several ambulances being called and periods of time in hospital. It was a very stressful time as we didn't know what was wrong and nothing seemed to help. That was the start of years of investigations before the diagnosis of non-epileptic attacks was given. A condition that presents itself like epilepsy but is caused from psychological stress and traumatic life events rather than physical factors.

Eggshells and Depression

Two years later I found myself pregnant with our sixth baby, which was a small miracle due to the distance between Mark and myself.

It was very clear to me that our marriage was not sustainable in the state that it was in. Despite the apologies and promises, things had got worse rather than better. Just hearing Mark's key in the door gave me a knot in my stomach as I waited to see what mood he was in. Would the kind caring Mark walk through the door, or would the angry unreasonable Mark be there?

Unfortunately it was rare that the Mark I had fallen in love with would appear. I was constantly tense and walking on eggshells, hoping that the explosion wouldn't happen. Not only did I not think that our marriage could continue in this way, I knew that *I* couldn't. I felt that I was losing my mind and felt so low at times, that I wondered if living was worth it.

It took being pregnant to finally see the doctor, something that I should have done years previously, and he diagnosed me with severe depression and put me on anti-depressants. Mark wasn't happy about it and told me that I had no reason to be depressed, my life was easy and that the doctor was wrong. Instead, he listed the awful things that had happened in his childhood and angrily stated that he should be the one on medication, so he booked himself an appointment with the doctor. Subsequently, the doctor told him that he was not depressed, but had an alcohol problem. He was offered help for his alcohol consumption but refused it.

Although Mark had been to different counsellors over the years to help him deal with his childhood experiences, we had never been together. Knowing that I was no longer able to cope with our relationship in the state that it was in, I suggested that we went to marriage counselling. A close friend recommended an experienced counsellor and Mark agreed to go.

After the first session, the counsellor said that he felt it would be more beneficial to see Mark by himself for a few weeks, before bringing us back together again, as Mark's issues were too deep to explore in a joint session. I don't know what they worked on but Mark seemed happier after each appointment and I felt some hope again that our marriage was worth saving.

Drunk Drama

At 33 weeks pregnant I was looking forward to the birth of my sixth baby to complete our family and I felt a hope for the future that I hadn't felt in a long time. I went to work on the Saturday afternoon after a relaxing family morning.

Turning my phone back on after work I had many missed calls and answering machine messages. Listening to the messages from my 13 year old made my heart stop. I heard fear and panic in her voice as she told me that she had called an ambulance because she thought her Dad had had a stroke.

I raced home to find an ambulance waiting and Mark inside, barely conscious and not speaking. The ambulance crew said his condition was a mystery to them and they were taking him to hospital. I didn't go with them, as I had nobody to watch my younger ones, but waited by the phone for news.

The waiting was awful. I stayed up late and hoped that Mark would be all right. Different scenarios were going through my mind and none of them were positive.

Finally, at eleven that night, the hospital rang and told me that they knew what was wrong with him. He was drunk. That was it. He was simply so drunk that he had fallen unconscious. They were releasing him home. I went from being scared and worried to angry. He had been in charge of two children under the age of five, as well as a thirteen year old, and had got so drunk that he needed hospital treatment. I felt as though all the promises and hope had been false.

Different scenarios played out in my head, but this time they were of my children coming to harm while he was paralytic. Thank goodness that my thirteen year old had been home to keep an eye on the younger ones. The thoughts of what might have happened if she hadn't been there were too awful.

When he returned home that night, he went straight to the spare room. I knew that there was still too much alcohol in his system to be able to discuss it, so I left him to sleep it off and tried to get some sleep myself, wondering if we had any future left.

The next morning I was already downstairs with the children when I heard movement from the spare room followed by footsteps heading to the front door. I went to the door and asked what he was doing to be told that he was going out to buy some cigarettes. I didn't question it any further as the local shop was only down the road and I expected him back in a few minutes. We could discuss the previous day when he returned.

Half an hour later he still hadn't returned and my anger that had been there from the previous night was growing. Instead of staying in waiting I decided to take the children to the park; I think I needed to get out of the house as much as them. But within 45 minutes of being at the park, my phone started going off. Friends started texting me to see if I had read Mark's Facebook status and to check that everything was all right. Taking a look at his status it read something like (and I can't remember the exact words), 'Nobody cares about me so I'm saying goodbye'.

It may seem odd, but I wasn't overly concerned as Mark would often leave the house and text me things like this after a row. A few years earlier I would have worried, but I knew that he wasn't serious and it was just one of his manipulative games.

When the police rang me to say that they were concerned for his welfare and wanted me to go home immediately I actually told them that I knew Mark wasn't serious, but they didn't know him like I did and took his threats to harm himself very seriously.

Over the next few hours different police officers came to the house to give me updates and ask me lots of personal questions about our marriage. They even searched the house for clues. This was probably the worst part as my privacy was invaded, as was the children's.

Finally, after nine hours, I heard footsteps on the stairs going into our bedroom. I went up and found Mark lying on the bed. I could see immediately that he was drunk and knew that it was not the moment for a confrontation, so I simply said that I had better tell the police that he was home. This was a mistake. He got very angry, started shouting and hitting the furniture. I rang 999 and explained what was happening while trying to keep the children calm.

Waiting for the police seemed to take forever. Mark had gone outside to have a cigarette but was smashing up some garden ornaments and punching the walls and doors. I stood in the doorway to make sure that he couldn't get back into the house and told the older children to take the little ones upstairs so they couldn't see what was happening. It was then that he turned his anger on the children, calling them names and swearing at them.

When the police came, he calmed down and became passive. I was worried that they wouldn't believe that he was a different person minutes earlier. However, they breathalysed him and found him nearly four times over the drink drive limit. One of the policeman told me that he wouldn't have believed that Mark was even drunk had he not seen the result. As Mark had driven home, he was arrested for drink driving and breach of the peace.

Two policemen came in to take a statement from me. While they were doing this, my thirteen year old said that her dad had lashed out at her the day before when he was drunk and as she tried to move him from the floor to the chair. She stated that his hand had hit her across the face. I was totally shocked and knew that this was different from the other times that he had been drunk and angry. This time, he had physically hurt one of our children.

The Beginning of the End

The policeman gently questioned her about the assault but as she wasn't sure whether it had been intentional or not, they didn't charge him with assault. However, it did result in them needing to contact the Multi-Agency Safeguarding Hub (MASH) team and social services, leading to a Multi-Agency Risk Assessment Conference (MARAC)[1] meeting and assessments by social services

---

[1] A MARAC is a meeting where information is shared on the highest risk domestic abuse cases in which it is assessed that a

over the following few weeks and months. I never thought that I would have been on that side of social services or would need meetings about how they were going to keep my children safe.

The following day the police rang to say that they were releasing him, but I told them I didn't want him to return to the home. I simply didn't know what our future held, but I did know that he wouldn't be coming back until he had got some help and stopped drinking. So the police drove him home to collect some belongings and escort him out.

The next morning I drove over to my sister-in-law's (which is where he was staying) to find the front door open, him almost unconscious, and an empty bottle next to him. I rang an ambulance as I was concerned he may have drunk enough to kill himself, but on arrival they said that he hadn't and there was nothing medically that they could do. They suggested that I got him to our doctors to see if he could give some long-term help.

They helped to get him in the back of my car and I drove him down there with him ranting the whole way. The doctor was great and told Mark exactly what the situation was. Basically, he told him to grow up, stop feeling sorry for himself and get some help if he wanted to keep his family. He turned to me and signed me off with stress until my maternity leave was due to start. He also suggested a place in town to get Mark some help, so I took Mark there with him ranting away and dragging his feet.

---

victim may be seriously harmed or killed. The meeting will involve representatives of local police, health, child protection, housing practitioners, Independent Domestic Violence Advisors (IDVAs), probation and other specialists from the statutory and voluntary sectors. After sharing all relevant information they have about a victim, the representatives discuss options for increasing the safety of the victim and turn these into a co-ordinated action plan. The primary focus of the MARAC is to safeguard the adult victim.

The place was for those addicted to alcohol and drugs and they were amazingly supportive to me as well as telling Mark some hard facts. They agreed that he should not come home until he was sober told him that he was a risk to the children and myself.

He was livid when they said this and started to get angry, so I was very glad that *they* had said it to him and not me. He explained that he wasn't a risk, even though he admitted hitting our daughter, stating that it wasn't his fault because he was drunk. The woman told him that it was totally his fault and that being drunk was not an excuse for assaulting a child. Even at this point, there was an excuse for his behaviour.

When social services came to do an assessment a couple of weeks later, I was told that had I kept Mark in the family home, my children would have been placed on the child protection register and could have been removed.

Despite not being together, I still felt that, as his wife, I should help him, so I made many phone calls to his friends, counsellors and professionals to try and get him help so that he could get sober and return to home, but nothing made any difference. I even hoped that the birth of our sixth baby might be the motivation to take responsibility for his actions.

Unfortunately, when our baby was just two days old, I had to ring 999 again as Mark turned up drunk and aggressive. On this occasion I had to physically push him out of the door as he was refusing to leave. Fortunately, all of our children, apart from our baby, were at school and nursery this time so they didn't have to witness it.

Mark didn't keep the appointment that was made with the alcohol team and declined further into drink to the point at which it was no longer safe for the children to see him at all. He was spending more time in custody and hospital (due to his drinking) than he was spending outside.

Finally Seeing the Truth

A few months later Mark broke into the house, stealing my credit card and the card to our joint account. Only my wages were going into that account but he withdrew £600 and blew it on a weekend of fun.

After that the police recommended that I should consult a solicitor and take out a non-molestation order, which I did. It meant that he couldn't contact me or go near the house. The police also installed a panic alarm as they felt that my children and I were at high risk of harm. It felt surreal. I couldn't understand why they were so concerned about our welfare. After all, Mark had never hit me, so I wasn't an abused wife.

It wasn't until a woman from the domestic abuse unit (that was attached to the police) spoke to me that I finally began to understand. She explained that, despite what I had believed, domestic abuse was not limited to physical violence. Talking through the years of our relationship, she helped me to see the mind games that he used, the manipulation tactics and his abusive behaviour. I reeled off the reasons that Mark had behaved in that way - childhood abuse, alcohol problems, stress at work etc - but she showed me that they weren't reasons, just excuses.

As Mark worked for the police he had been able to persuade me that his actions were not abusive, and I had believed him. Now, a professional working for the police was explaining how he had used his position to be able to obscure me from seeing what was really happening. As he worked for the police, they were also particularly concerned for me as they felt Mark knew how to play the system, which is why they had taken the extra steps of installing a panic alarm and referring my case to MARAC.

I always saw myself as a strong, independent woman who was intelligent and held a professional position as a teacher. Yet, I had been emotionally and mentally abused for years, without even knowing it. I knew that I was hurting, felt confused, depressed, scared, worried and doubted my own mind, but I didn't think that it was abuse because he told me it wasn't.

No matter what job you have, how strong you are, whether you are male or female, it is possible to be abused. But, it is also possible to be free of abuse and love life again.

2
WHEN HURT IS ABUSE

Domestic violence and abuse. These words evoke a range of responses and perceptions. Some may be a result of the media, widespread myths or personal experiences.

Personally, my idea of domestic abuse was of a man who hit his wife on a regular basis. I wasn't in that type of relationship. My ex-husband had never hit me. I expect that many have this view. Yet, physical abuse is only one type of abuse that happens behind closed doors.

Domestic abuse can take many forms:

- psychological
- physical
- sexual
- financial
- emotional

Despite not hitting me, he would use his physical body to stand in a doorway and refuse to let me leave the room while shouting at me, or use his physical size to intimidate me and punch a wall close to me.

If I said that he couldn't do that, he would tell me that he wasn't doing anything wrong because he hadn't laid a finger on me and never would. My ex-husband worked for the police. I believed him when he said that it wasn't abuse. But I shouldn't have. It was finally the police that made me see that I was a victim of domestic abuse and that I had been for years.

These are the signs of domestic violence according to Women's Aid:[2]

- **Destructive criticism and verbal abuse**: shouting/mocking/accusing/name calling/verbally threatening.

- **Pressure tactics**: sulking, threatening to withhold money, disconnect the telephone, take the car away, commit suicide, take the children away, report you to welfare agencies unless you comply with his demands regarding bringing up the children, lying to your friends and family about you, telling you that you have no choice in any decisions.

- **Disrespect**: persistently putting you down in front of other people, not listening or responding when you talk, interrupting your telephone calls, taking money from your purse without asking, refusing to help with childcare or housework.

- **Breaking trust**: lying to you, withholding information from you, being jealous, having other relationships, breaking promises and shared agreements.

- **Isolation:** monitoring or blocking your telephone calls, telling you where you can and cannot go, preventing you from seeing friends and relatives.

- **Harassment**: following you, checking up on you,

[2] www.womensaid.org.uk/information-support/what-is-domestic-abuse/recognising-domestic-abuse

opening your mail, repeatedly checking to see who has telephoned you, embarrassing you in public.

- **Threats**: making angry gestures, using physical size to intimidate, shouting you down, destroying your possessions, breaking things, punching walls, wielding a knife or a gun, threatening to kill or harm you and the children.

- **Physical violence**: punching, slapping, hitting, biting, pinching, kicking, pulling hair out, pushing, shoving, burning, strangling.

- **Denial**: saying the abuse doesn't happen, saying you caused the abusive behaviour, being publicly gentle and patient, crying and begging for forgiveness, saying it will never happen again.

My ex-husband didn't do all of these, but he did more than half of them. A partner doesn't have to do all of these for it to be abuse.

I expect some people would wonder why I stayed married for so long, so I will try to explain.

Firstly, because there was no physical violence, I believed him when he said that it wasn't domestic violence and it wasn't that bad. After all, everyone has their ups and downs in a marriage.

Secondly, as part of this, I was in denial. I wanted to believe that it wasn't that bad. Or that it was the drink. Or his abusive childhood. Or the range of reasons that he gave me. It is sometimes easier to be in denial than to face reality.

Thirdly, I believe that I am a positive person and I always try to see the best of every situation. Unfortunately, even after I realised that things were not 'normal' my positivity gave me hope that he could be 'cured'. I persuaded him to talk to several people, friends and professionals, about his issues in the hope that once these were dealt with he would be 'better'.

Fourthly, a lot of the abuse was emotional and psychological. He would threaten suicide, walk out for hours, say that he would fight me for custody, tell me sob stories and generally use a range of tactics to make me stay.

Fifthly, I loved him, and I believed that when you love someone, you try to help them and to give them another chance.

Finally, it wasn't all bad. He wasn't abusive every day or every week. It was like living with a Jekyll and Hyde character. He could be very loving — saying kind words or buying me little gifts. But you never knew whether it would be Jekyll or Hyde that walked through the door each day. And you never knew what would change him from one to the other, so there was a lot of walking on eggshell.

Even after we split up he still had a hold on me. I offered to give him money for a deposit on a flat, which he took but lost when he was evicted after getting drunk. I drove him to the doctors and support workers to get him help. I organised places for him to stay and facilitated the contact between him and our children.

I remember talking to one of the domestic abuse support team and telling her that I was going to speak to our local contact centre to arrange supervised access for him to see our younger three children. She told me that he was still emotionally controlling me, even though he had left. She firmly stated that if he wanted to see his children, then he should be the one to organise it. After all, I was trying to take care of six children, the family finances and returning back to work. So, I never made that phone call. And guess what? Neither did he.

It is hard to see that it is happening when you are in that situation. Fortunately, I am now out of the relationship and free to make my own decisions without being lied to, abused or manipulated.

Now I hope to help others to see through the fog of confusion and inner conflict, so that they can break free from power and control.

3
USING HIS BODY

In the same way that a partner doesn't have to carry out all of the signs of domestic abuse (from the previous chapter) for them to be abusing you, they don't have to be using all of the tactics that I will be discussing in this chapter. You may not recognise these behaviours as being abusive, despite the hurt that they cause you, but that's what your partner wants — to hide the fact that it is abuse.

Using his body may mean physically hitting, pushing or kicking as in a friend's relationship:

I was so shocked the first time he hit me. I didn't know what to think. His face was angry one moment and then the next he was crying and saying sorry over and over again. I really believed him when he said that he would never hurt me again.

Months later, he slapped me across the face, but I thought it was my fault. I had made him angry by asking why he was late home from work. He made me feel guilty. He told me he was feeling insecure and I felt sorry for him. I believed I could help him and make him better so we could have the relationship that we used to have, before he hit me.

Sadly, the beliefs that a partner will not do it again or will change, are common but will very rarely be justified. Instead, it is a shocking fact that 1 in 4 women in violent relationships receive substantial injuries.[3]

Most violence in a relationship doesn't start with substantial injuries, but rather with a push, shove or slap before increasing over time. It is this gradual build up of violence, along with tranquil and loving periods in the relationship, that makes it difficult for the woman to see her relationship as abusive. Instead, she will often stay to help her partner or to provide the children with a family unit.

Quite often though, as in my marriage, there isn't any physical contact in an abusive relationship, yet he will still use his body to physically intimidate and control his partner.

Rather than physically pushing or hitting me, Mark would look angry, go red in the face, grit his teeth, glare at me and clenching his fists. There were also incidents when he would place his hands either side of me when I was next to a wall to cage me in. Other times, he would stop me leaving the room by using his body as a barricade.

The anger was visible through this body language and caused fear as I sensed that Mark was about to explode.

Other methods that he may use are to stand over his partner, puffing out his chest aggressively while shouting at her with his face almost touching hers or using his body as a barrier to keep her trapped and making her feel dominated.

Smashing up possessions, slamming doors or punching walls are all further examples of ways in which he can use his body to create fear and anxiety without actually coming into physical contact with her. He can then tell her that he is not like other men out there who hit their partners, to make her feel as though she is lucky not to be with anyone else who may actually hurt her.

---

[3] Crime Survey of England and Wales 2013/14

The lack of physical contact also stops her reporting it or seeking help. The term 'domestic violence' suggests that there needs to be a physical injury and if there is no physical contact, then he has done nothing wrong. However, anyone using their physical body to scare, intimidate or control their partner, is physically abusing them.

4
USING HIS WORDS

Sticks and stones may break my bones, but words will never hurt me.

This playground nursery rhyme is often said as a retort to verbal taunting or bullying and suggests that a verbal attack doesn't hurt in the same way as a physical one. Yet, I'm sure that anyone who has been verbally attacked will know that this is simply untrue.

Words may not leave physical bruises and scars, but they do leave scars on our mind that can hurt us over and over again as we replay them. Verbal abuse is certainly no less damaging than physical abuse, although it is often more difficult to recognise because it is subtle, private and can take many forms. It is also harder to quantify and prove.

Name Calling

There are many forms of verbal abuse, with the most obvious being name calling, for example, idiot, fat, dummy, bitch, whore, which is often done in angry outbursts. This may be done in public to shame a partner in front of others, but is more often done in the privacy of home so that the perpetrator can maintain the image of being a perfect partner in public. When name calling is done privately, it is secretive and more confusing because the name-caller is one person in public and a different one in private. Who would believe that the loving partner can also be a verbal abuser? So, it often stays hidden behind closed doors even though name calling is clearly abusive.

Subtle Manipulation

However, other forms of verbal abuse are less evident and are harder to recognise in a relationship. They are subtle, easy to misinterpret, manipulative, don't use anger and don't seem to fit the common view of abuse. These forms of verbal abuse can make the partner question herself, wondering if she is overreacting or being oversensitive. She may even feel as though she is going crazy, especially when it builds up over time so that she doesn't recognise that it is happening.

In my relationship with Mark I often felt as though I was losing my mind. He would say something and then deny it minutes or hours later. Over time I began to question my own memory (or lack of it) and would try to replay the original conversation in my mind to recall what was actually said. With every denial, I doubted my own mind further and reality became distorted.

This increased when we had an argument. He would deliberately start a row, twist my words and contradict himself, leaving me feeling as though I was going crazy. A typical argument would go like this:

Mark: *I can't stand how some people get extra money from my hard-earned taxes for made up disabilities like ADHD.*

Me: *There are a lot of doctors that think ADHD does exist though.*

Mark: *No, there isn't. No doctor would diagnosis a made up thing.*

Me: *Well, they have because we know x and her daughter has been diagnosed.*

Mark: *Yes, I know that she has ADHD. I'm not stupid.*

Me: *I didn't say that you were but ADHD must be being diagnosed if x daughter has a diagnosis.*

Mark: *Of course I know that it is being diagnosed. How stupid do you think I am?*

Me: *So it's not made up then?*

Mark: (angrily) *I never said it was.*

At the end of an interaction like this I would feel as though I wasn't living in reality as nothing made sense. I couldn't express an opinion or have a discussion with Mark because he would deny saying things, counteract anything I said and contradict himself. His viewpoint was constantly changing and so there was no way to know what he really thought.

It was abusive because it dismissed my feelings and opinions, it was done to cause me to question my reality and it destroyed communication in our relationship.

There are many subtle ways that a partner can be verbally abusive that I will describe, but the one common factor is that they are all mentally and emotionally damaging with the goal to control and manipulate.

The Silent Treatment

A partner may refuse to speak to the other so that she questions what she has done wrong, replaying events and words that led up to the silence, or being worried for her partner's state of mind. Using silence gives him the power by making her desperate to know what the problem is and wanting to fix it. It's the opposite of blowing up and shouting, yet still produces a tense and dark atmosphere within the house and within the other partner.

Withholding any form of communication is damaging to relationships as it prevents an exchange of feelings and thoughts, destroying the intimacy of the relationship. She can end up feeling alone rather than in a partnership and left wondering what she has done wrong to alienate and hurt her partner.

Counteracting

This may take the shape of counteracting her opinions, even if he agrees with her. Or arguing that he hates a television programme that she enjoys when he does actually enjoy watching it too. This is often done to cause a disagreement and create a gap in their relationship, as she can't keep track with his opinions that constantly change. It results in not knowing who your partner is and what they are thinking, destroying the foundations of a relationship.

It was only a Joke

Sometimes a partner may disguise verbal abuse as a joke. For example, saying that she is fat or a bad driver, but if she gets upset adding on, "Aw, it was only a joke".

If the joke is hurtful (and fully intended that way) then it is abusive. Constant joking about characteristics of a partner is belittling and leads to her self-esteem gradually diminishing, usually without her realising it. In fact, verbal abuse often begins with what appears to be harmless jokes.

It's all your Fault

Accusing the other partner of starting it all, or blaming her for his actions, are also methods of verbal abuse. He may accuse his partner of causing the argument, of over-reacting, or of making things up. So instead of him being the instigator of the disagreement, he shifts the blame to his partner, putting her on the defensive.

In my relationship I often felt as though I was having to defend myself without knowing why. A simple discussion would somehow result in me reassuring Mark and apologising for any hurt that I had caused although I didn't know what I had said to cause a problem. Now I can see that I didn't say anything to hurt Mark but he twisted it so that I would feel that I was to blame.

He may also directly blame his partner for the problems rather than taking responsibility himself. For example, "I wouldn't be angry and we wouldn't be having this argument if you had listened to me/done what I asked/been less selfish". By moving the blame for their actions from themselves to their partner, they are deflecting their responsibility.

Being Put Down

In a relationship, each partner should be trying to raise each other up. In an abusive relationship, one partner is trying to have power over the other and one way is through judging and criticising. By putting someone down you raise yourself up.

Often comments aren't obviously critical, making it hard to see what is really being meant underneath. "Have you still not finished that task?" "You're not very good with money, so I will look after the finances from now on." "Why are you upset? You have so many insecurities that it is hard to love you." These are subtle ways to make her feel as though she isn't good enough and doubt her own abilities and strength.

Threats

Words can also be used to threaten a partner. The most obvious threats are those of physical harm, but there are also more subtle ways of threatening a partner that are less easy to recognise. These are more likely to be implied.

As I explained previously, Mark would suggest that he was going to commit suicide after an argument by walking out of the house, sending a text, such as *'Goodbye'* and leaving me to worry for hours, with the knowledge that he had previously made a suicide attempt. I remember telling a friend that I could never leave him as he might harm himself and I wouldn't be able to live with the guilt. Threatening suicide was his way to stop me leaving him, but I only realized this after we had split up.

Threats can be implied and manipulative as well as more direct. Both are a means of control and power so that the partner will feel that they have to do something that they don't wish to because of the potential consequences.

Lack of Appreciation

Everyone wants to feel appreciated and be acknowledged in a relationship. However, some partners will do the opposite of this. Instead of making positive comments about something their partner has done or said, they will make it seem worthless or unimportant. Again, this widens the gap in the relationship as she becomes reluctant to convey her achievements to him because she fears he will take her positive feelings away.

Within my relationship Mark would often fail to acknowledge things that I had done and instead take credit for them. For example, when I received a high mark on one of my degree essays, I showed it to him, but he turned away and said that I should thank him for my mark because he was the one who took the children to the park for a couple of hours so that I could write it without distractions. Over time, I stopped telling him about things that I was proud of as he would never be positive about it and instead, would turn it around so that I would have to praise him. Not having things that you have done appreciated, or even acknowledged, results in feeling under-valued and insignificant in the relationship.

As we have seen verbal abuse can come in many forms, and many are hard to recognise, especially when you are in the relationship. The common factor is that verbal abuse is done to intentionally hurt the other partner and is done over a period of time to wear down the other partner and erode the relationship.

5
USING YOUR EMOTIONS

Like verbal abuse, emotional abuse isn't evident through physical marks and like verbal abuse, it results in psychological scars that can last a lifetime.

There is a strong overlap between verbal and emotional abuse as both use words to have the power in the relationship. Verbal abuse can also be emotional abuse because it is intended to cause emotional pain. I won't repeat the examples of verbal abuse from the previous chapter, but many of those discussed are also examples of emotional abuse.

Emotional abuse is as damaging as physical abuse and it affects how she sees herself. Underlying emotional abuse is manipulation. One partner uses mind games to manipulate the other. Using manipulation gives him the power and control that he craves. On the other hand, she feels as if she is going crazy, loses her confidence, happiness and self-esteem, grows fearful and unsure of reality.

Emotional abuse develops over time, with him slowly breaking her down. So slowly that she doesn't even notice it happening until she is at the point of breaking.

I'm going to give some examples of emotional abuse that I experienced to help others recognise it, but emotional abuse can take so many forms (depending on the person) that this isn't an exhaustive list. If you are experiencing behaviour from your partner that makes you feel humiliated, unworthy, guilty, unsure of yourself, confused, fearful, lonely or rejected, then it could be emotional abuse.

Twisting and Turning

Some people seem to be able to twist and turn the truth so that it is no longer possible tell what is the truth and what are lies. An abuser may twist things to justify his behaviour and actions.

For example, most evenings (unless he already had some in the house) Mark would go out to buy four of cans of beer, although I was unaware that he was actually buying far more than that. He would also buy me a chocolate bar or a bag of sweets and give them to me. If I then complained about Mark spending money, that we didn't have, on alcohol he would say that I had no right to say that as I was spending money on chocolate and sweets. Explaining that I didn't buy the chocolate or sweets, or even ask him to do so, he would twist it around to either say that I was ungrateful for his presents and he wouldn't bother being nice again, or he would insist that I had asked him to.

Rather than focusing on his actions of spending the money on alcohol, he had twisted it to either make me seem ungrateful and the wrongdoer or that I was just as bad by wanting him to spend money on me. Both of these moved the focus from him to me. He had twisted it so that I was in the wrong and he was the one in the right.

Finally, it gets to the stage where she knows that there is no point saying anything as it will get turned around, making her feel as though she is wrong and is hurting him, rather than the other way around.

By twisting and turning the truth she starts to question whether she is actually the one in the wrong and if she has remembered things accurately. It leads to her replaying past events and words in her mind, in the hope of finding the truth. This uses a lot of mental and emotional energy. Finally, she may give up and stop expressing her concerns about his behaviour and actions, which gives him the green light to continue doing what he is doing.

Projection

Projection is a defence method in which someone will attribute characteristics they find unacceptable in themselves to someone else. For example, he may smash items in the house when they have a row but would accuse her of having an anger problem if she shouts for him to stop.

For the partner who is being accused, it can lead her to start questioning whether it is her that is at fault. She may doubt herself, feel confused and start thinking that she is the one who has the problem. In the example given, she may agree that she was angry when she shouted at him to stop and so think that it is her that has the problem that needs resolving rather than him.

If she knows that she is innocent of his accusations she will face a difficult struggle to prove her innocence. For him to agree that she is innocent will mean that he will have to admit to himself, and her, that he is at fault. Rather than being accountable he would prefer to shift the blame onto her through projection.

When Mark left the family home Social Services were satisfied that I was safeguarding our children from the emotional abuse that he had used on both them and myself. It was only the fact that I refused to let him back home that Social Services closed the case. Yet, since our marriage break-up, Mark has accused me of emotionally abusing our children and being a bad mother. It might seem easy to dismiss the accusations but he built up a case which made me sit down and consider whether I was doing the right thing by our children, or whether I was also emotionally abusing them. So, despite having no direct contact with him in over two years, Mark still managed to make me question and doubt myself.

It is only because I'm no longer regularly having his behaviour projected onto me, and I am out of the situation, that I could recognise what he was doing and stop my self-examination.

Other ways that he could project his issues are by making statements about her that are really about himself. For example, "You have no compassion for my feelings". In reality, she is probably bending over backwards for him, while he isn't thinking about her at all. Or, "You're selfish", when the reality is that he is the selfish one, putting his needs above hers.

Turning Good Things into Bad

Mark would often start an argument over nothing just to be able to shout and rage. Over time I noticed that these would be worse before or after a positive event, such as Christmas, weddings, even a first scan of our baby. Any event that should have left a happy memory was turned sour.

All abuse is to do with power and control, so spoiling something that makes her happy is having power over her emotions. It also results in an emotional roller coaster in which she can be ecstatic one moment and trying to work out why she's being shouted at in the next. Being on an emotional roller coaster is exhausting in itself, but also throw in some verbal abuse and mind games, and it is no wonder that there is no fight back left. He has ruined her happiness and left her feeling confused and vulnerable. Each time he does it, he breaks her spirit a bit more and she may even start to stop herself feeling happy when she should do because she knows that he will begin to be abusive.

Playing the Victim Card

From the first day that we met Mark portrayed himself as a victim. First, a victim of an uncaring wife who had an affair and then left him homeless and penniless. Then, a victim of abuse within the family, before telling me about abuse from people outside of the family. At this early stage of the relationship, Mark being a victim made him appear vulnerable and harmless. He needed someone to love and support him. He certainly didn't seem able to be abusive himself.

Playing the victim was a tactic that remained throughout our relationship, although the perpetrator changed. Instead of his ex-wife or family, it became the alcohol, myself, the stress of the job or the children that were the cause of the problems. He continued to be the victim who felt sorry for himself.

The partner who plays the victim card is refusing to take on any responsibility or accountability. Instead, he is passing the blame onto his partner, another person or life event.

Being a victim continued when Mark left. Within three days of leaving, he had been diagnosed with Post Traumatic Stress Disorder (PTSD) through an online questionnaire sent by a therapist. The caring side of me wanted to take him back. After all, he wasn't doing it to be cruel, he had a mental illness. Fortunately friends helped me to see what was really going on. He was playing on my caring side to come back and rather than accept that it was him that had caused pain to our family, he blamed the PTSD.

Even after the breakdown of our marriage and involvement of the police and social services due to Mark's behaviour, he still portrayed himself as the victim. It was never his fault.

Since then he has claimed to have had a range of mental and physical illnesses. More recently he claimed to have cancer and months to live, begging me to let him see the children. I have since found out that he had a stomach ulcer and never had cancer. But with the lack of cancer came claims of heart attacks and strokes. Fortunately, I can see through the charade now. But in previous years, I fell for the victim story.

Most people would feel for someone who was a victim of others' actions or circumstances, so when he plays the victim card rather than acknowledging that his behaviour or actions are wrong, it is natural for her to want to care for and look after him instead of confronting him about his behaviour.

This is how the manipulation of playing the victim card works. Rather than being able to focus on and deal with his behaviour or actions, she feels that she needs to support and care for him (as the 'victim') instead. She may even feel that she is the cause of his unhappiness, or he may have directly blamed her. It is incredibly difficult not to see him as the victim, but instead see him as the one doing the abusing.

Saying Sorry (but not meaning it)

Linked to playing the victim is when a partner will say sorry for his behaviour and then follow it with a direct or an implied 'but'. For example, "I am really sorry that I lost control then, but you know that I am stressed at work and so shouldn't have asked me that, but I am sorry".

Or, "I know that I am a terrible husband and you deserve so much better. If only I could stop drinking then I would be the man you deserve".

Or, "I'm really sorry that I yelled at you like that. It's been a bad day at work. You wouldn't believe how stressful it is. I know I shouldn't take it out on you but you're the only one here that I can share it with. I couldn't manage without you".

In these examples, there has been no accepting of responsibility for his own actions and so is not a genuine apology. He has held her accountable in the first example, drink accountable in the second example and stress in the third. Furthermore, in the final example, he has turned the situation around so that she may feel guilty for bringing up his behaviour as he starts flattering her. Rather than him feeling remorse at his actions, and accepting the responsibility to change, he has shifted it so that she feels responsible for him.

Without genuine acceptance of responsibility and a change of behaviour as a result, apologies are simply words said to get her to forgive and forget. If she won't let it go and forgive, she will be viewed as the one at fault rather than him. Shifting the guilt and shame away from himself and onto her, leaving her feeling unworthy of his love.

As a Christian, I felt pressure to forgive Mark no matter what he did because I felt it was what God expected me to do: "For if you forgive men when they sin against you, your heavenly Father will also forgive you. But if you do not forgive men their sins, your Father will not forgive your sins." (Matthew 6:14-15, NIV.) However, forgiving someone so that you can let go of anger, and allowing someone to continue to abuse you are two separate things.

Righteousness

I'm far from perfect and don't want anyone to think that I'm claiming to be so. Like most people I can admit when I don't know something or I've made a mistake. However, in some relationships a partner will be righteous and act as though he is above everyone else.

Mark acted superior a lot. Just watching the news on the television could spark a rant at 'those people who were bringing society down'. At home he wouldn't listen to others' opinions. He was right and everyone else was wrong even though it flew in the face of reason.

Trying to have discussions about issues or concerns with someone who thinks they are always right and superior, is almost impossible. Instead of listening to the other person's point of view, they will only see their own viewpoint. Expressing your own thoughts and feelings can seem as pointless as talking to a brick wall, which destroys the intimacy of the relationship.

You're So Perfect

Shifting from being righteous to accusing the other partner of being righteous is another tactic that is used to confuse and manipulate emotions. For example:

A: "Could you stop coming into the lounge with your muddy shoes on please?"
B: "You think you're so perfect, don't you?"
A: "No, I don't."
B: "Well you must be because you're sat there criticising me."
A: "I'm not perfect. I was just trying to…"
B: "No you're right. I'm a useless idiot and you deserve better than me. You could get anyone you wanted. But what about me. Nobody would want me. I'm ugly and thick."
A: "No you're not. I never said that. I was just trying to…"
B: "If you really think like that I'll leave. You can explain to the kids why you're chucking me out. I'll just go and pack now, shall I?"
A: "No I'm sorry. I didn't mean it. Please don't go."

By accusing her of being perfect and criticising himself, she feels drawn to negate his negative comments about himself. Rather than being able to discuss an issue, she is reassuring him and begging him to stay. He is the one who is name-calling (by calling her perfect) and even though it appears to be a positive comment, it is a manipulative tool to put her on the defensive. Afterwards, she may wonder how the conversation moved from her making a simple request to her asking him not to leave her.

In Denial

When he denies that events or interactions happened, even though both partners know that they did, it causes her to question her reality. It may be denying that he said something or it could be denying that she cooked for him the previous night. Over time, these denials cause her to become unsure of her own mind, so that she doubts her own memories.

I know that I became so confused with Mark's denials of things that I threatened to record conversations to prove to both of us that I wasn't remembering things incorrectly or making them up.

This caused an explosive reaction so I was too afraid to actually do it.

Jekyll and Hyde

I would often feel that my marriage to Mark was like being married to Jekyll and Hyde. The difficulty was that I never knew which one would come home from work or when he would change from one to another. This meant I was walking on eggshells, hoping that nothing I or the children did would turn him into the aggressive and unreasonable Hyde. Often I had no idea what had caused a change of mood or what would turn a pleasant evening together into one in which I couldn't say or do anything right.

It was this constant uncertainty of not knowing who I would be dealing with from day to day (or moment to moment) that would leave a knotted sensation in my stomach every time I heard his key in the front door. That feeling wouldn't reduce until he was asleep or had gone out. It was only after Mark left the family home and I had a non-molestation order to ensure that he didn't return, that I relaxed and realised how tense I had been.

Keeping his partner unsure, anxious and worried gives him the power and control over her emotions. It also slowly breaks her emotionally as she ends up exhausted and on constant alert.

Possessiveness

Emotional abuse can come in the form of a partner being possessive of his partner. This can slowly creep into the relationship as he tries to isolate her from friends and family so that she is totally his.

It may be done subtly at first by making comments such as, "Surely you want to spend time with me?" if she has arranged to meet her friends. Or, he may arrive at her house unannounced, with a takeaway, on an evening that he knew she was going out for a family meal so that she feels she has to stay in with him instead.

In the early part of a relationship, possessiveness may also be expressed as a concern for her well-being. For example, concern that she might be attacked on the walk home, so he insists on collecting her at a certain time from a particular place. Or, he may be concerned that she is doing too much and will end up tired, so suggests she cuts down on some activities and hobbies.

Over time it may be more direct and he may simply state that she is not to go out with her friends and family. He may even start putting up barriers between her and those she cares for by causing issues when he sees them, making false accusations about them or criticising them to her.

I used to work in a shop in the earlier part of our marriage. Mark often finished work before I did, in which case he would pop in to see me. If he couldn't physically pop in, he would phone up just to have a chat.

At first this was lovely and I thought that it showed how much he cared, but it got to a point when it was so often that it started seeming strange. Nobody else's partners phoned or came into the shop. It started to feel uncomfortable and I could tell my manager was starting to get a little annoyed as it took me away from serving customers.

When I explained this to Mark he didn't take it well, accusing me of not wanting to see him. Even accusing me of having an affair with one of the other staff. I quickly dropped the topic as it was clear that he wasn't going to stop contacting me at work and all I was doing was causing an argument.

Being possessive and jealous destroys the trust in a relationship as well as keeping the other partner trapped. It has no place in a healthy relationship. Being possessive is not treating the other partner as an equal but as though she is a possession to be owned and ultimately controlled.

6
USING MONEY

Financial abuse is less spoken about than physical, verbal or emotional abuse, yet it often co-exists alongside them. This abuse is also to control a partner, and can leave her feeling isolated and unable to escape.

Financial Control

The way this abuse manifests itself can vary depending on the partners and their situation, but it is all about control over finances. It may be that one partner likes to control all decisions regarding how the money is spent. He may happily spend money for his own benefit and enjoyment, but not allow her to spend money on herself. For example, Mark would spend money every day on alcohol, yet rant about the cost of my haircut (which would be around £25) and what a waste of money it was. So I only had my hair cut every 6-8 months because I knew I was going to get criticised for it.

Controlling how the money is spent can also mean that he takes care of all the household finances; "I'll take care of the bills. You don't have to worry about it". This sounds as though he is being caring by taking away some stress from her, but in a relationship everything, including finances, should be transparent rather than one partner controlling the expenditure. When it isn't transparent and openly discussed, one partner is holding the financial power and dominating the relationship.

Alternatively, a partner may withhold money and give an allowance to his partner. This is more like to happen if he works and she doesn't. It may be a mutual decision for her to stay at home to look after their young children or he may have insisted that it would be better for her to be at home while he worked. Regardless of who works, one partner shouldn't use finances to control the other partner. Withholding money is controlling and gives one partner power over the other.

He may say phrases such as, "I'm better at saving, so let's put the money in my account" which looks as though he's thinking about both of them by saving, but he's actually suggesting that she is bad with money. By putting the finances into an account that is just in his name and not joint names, means that she can't access it and he has the power over that money even if she has contributed to the savings.

Stealing money is not something that you would expect to happen in a marriage, however sadly, it does happen. A partner may know his partner's pin number and withdraw cash from her account without her knowledge or consent. Or he may use her credit/debit card to purchase items on line. If she later questions it, he may say that he spent it on the household, buying food or paying bills, so she feels that she can't complain that he stole it.

He may keep assets such as property in his name, which leaves her feeling as though she is living in his house and that she owns nothing, despite contributing to the mortgage each month. This leads to uncertainty about leaving a relationship because she will have nowhere to live. By holding assets in his name and denying her any financial security, she faces a difficult decision as to whether to leave and face homelessness or stay in an abusive relationship.

Financial Debt

Whereas some abusers don't allow their partners to have any say in the household finances and control every penny, other abusers trap their partners with mountains of debt, putting all the household bills in their name, taking out loans in joint names or insisting that the partner pays more than her fair share of the bills.

In the last months of our marriage, Mark stated that as a marriage was supposed to be equal, our finances should be equal. It sounded fair at this stage until he said that we should split all the bills equally and each pay our half. As I had two children under 5 who were at home, we had previously decided that it didn't make financial sense to be paying all of my wages to a nursery so that I could go to work full-time.

Therefore, I was working 3 days a week compared to Mark's full-time position. I had only half the income that Mark had and so it would have been impossible to split the bills equally. What it would have meant was that I would have had to get into debt to pay my half of the bills, whereas Mark would have had surplus income to spend on whatever he wished.

This particular situation played on my mind a lot as I did want an equal relationship and so felt that I should do my share. Mark was also very persuasive in his argument that splitting the bills would be fairer because he was feeling the pressure of supporting both of us. He made me feel so guilty for being at home more than him that I finally agreed. Before the new arrangement started we split up, so I never paid half but I know I would have done.

There can be a lot of lies in a financially abusive relationship. One partner might have a lot of debt, and the other may have no knowledge of it until it comes to the point of debt collection agencies being involved or the couple separating.

If the other partner is aware of the debt, then she may have been persuaded to put her name on a loan to pay it off (as I was), meaning that she is jointly liable. This can cause financial repercussions if they do decide to end the relationship and he leaves her with the debts. By having debts in joint names, she will be equally responsible for making the repayments or face difficulties getting credit in the future.

Financial abuse, like the other types of abuse discussed, is purely about power and control. Either he wants to have all the control over the finances or he wants the power to relieve himself of some of the burden, transferring it to her, and making her feel trapped.

The effect of financial abuse can be a lack of trust in the future over financial affairs, becoming trapped in poverty and/or debt, a lack of confidence and feelings of isolation. All of which can keep the woman in the abusive relationship, or have an impact on her life for a long time after it ends.

SECTION 3 – WHY DO THEY DO IT?

When you are being hurt in a relationship, the big question that you keep returning to is why.

Why do they keep hurting me?

Why don't they stop?

Why can't they see what it is doing to me?

Why don't they seem to feel the same emotions that I am?

Why do they say they will change and then do it again?

Why did they say they loved me when they hurt me?

7
THEIR PAST

A common perception is that children who are abused are more likely to abuse as an adult because it has become learned behaviour. There has certainly been numerous studies on this possible correlation.

The World Health Organisation Regional Office for Europe has produced a report on the cycle of violence and found that there is a link between being maltreated as a child and becoming an abuser as an adult, but it is not inevitable:

"The consensus from research is that individuals with a history of abuse in childhood are at increased risk of maltreating their own children and/or partners...However, this intergenerational pathway of maltreatment is not inevitable.[4]"

In fact, they found that "Research evidence shows that people who were abused as children have a higher probability of living with a

---

[4]

www.euro.who.int/_data/assets/pdf_file/0008/98783/E90619.pd f violent spouse". In other words, being abused as a child increases the chance of being abused as an adult.

So, being in an abusive home as a child does increase the risk of becoming an abuser as an adult, but it also increases the risk of being a victim.

Being subjected to abuse by a parent doesn't mean that it is inevitable that a person will abuse their partner or children. It is a choice to abuse.

Some partners will blame their childhood for their actions. They will portray themselves as a victim. They will ask for understanding and want their partner to care for them.

While I am not denying the fact that adult survivors of child abuse need comfort, encouragement and love, sadly some will use past abuse as part of a mind game to emotionally abuse their partner.

In my relationship, Mark would frequently refer to the physical abuse that he suffered at the hands of his mother and brother when he was a child. He was very open about it and, upon meeting new people, would often tell them about the abuse within a short space of time. Mark saw himself as a victim of abuse and never a perpetrator of abuse. As a victim he would use his past as an excuse for his behaviour, stating that it wasn't his fault that he was messed up in the head and couldn't control himself. Or he would state that his explosive rages around the home were due to his anger towards his mother and brother.

As a result, the focus moved from Mark's outbursts to me offering comfort and empathy to him for his past. I was left feeling guilty for feeling hurt about his actions because he persuaded me that he was hurting far more than I was.

Adult survivors of child abuse need professional support and assistance to work through the past. They shouldn't only be relying on their partner as a means of support as a partner is not a professional counsellor. Also it could negatively impact on their relationship as their roles become victim and supporter rather than an equally supportive, intimate relationship.

Being a victim of child abuse in the past does not excuse abusing a partner or a child in the present. Nor does it provide a partner a means to shift the responsibility for his own abusive behaviour onto his past.

8
ALCOHOL

Mark had to drink every evening. He said that it was just a couple of cans a night. He said that a couple of cans a night was normal behaviour for most men. He said that I should be grateful that he didn't go to the pub and get drunk like other men.

What I didn't know was that when he used to go outside to smoke, he would also consume more alcohol. After he left, I found his secret hiding place where there were hundreds of bottles and cans. There is no doubt in my mind that he was an alcoholic.

Previously, he had admitted to having a drinking problem and had even been to Alcoholics Anonymous twice, before claiming to be 'cured' which he said meant he could manage his drinking. Him admitting the problem meant that I stayed with him to help him get better. But I now know that it was just part of the manipulation and that they were empty words.

A common belief about domestic abuse is that it is linked to alcohol. There is a range of evidence that shows that alcohol is often present in domestic abuse incidents. One study found that 73% of perpetrators of reported domestic violence incidents had been drinking at the time of a physical assault.[5]

However, it is also clear that not everyone who drinks will abuse their partner. Most people who have a drink of alcohol don't abuse their partner. Equally, not all people who do abuse their partners have had an alcoholic drink.

Undeniably, alcohol affects our mood, perceptions and inhibitions but, alcohol will not generally turn a non-abusive person into a violent and abusive one.

Dr. David Calcutta suggests that rather than simply linking alcohol and violence, there may be a number of personality factors—such as irritability, poor anger control, and low levels of empathy — that lead certain people to become aggressive while drunk. Caldicott suggests that these are the same types of people who would behave aggressively while sober too. Alcohol just serves as a catalyst for this behaviour because it impairs the brain's executive system — the parts of the brain used in decision making and problem solving. The more intoxicated someone becomes, the harder time they have thinking about the consequences of their actions, which in some cases can lead to violent behaviour.

Alcohol doesn't change someone's personality or moral compass. Alcohol may increase the severity or frequency of abusive behaviour but someone who is not abusive when sober will not change into an abusive partner after drinking alcohol.

However, a partner may use the alcohol as an excuse for their actions.

Mark's explosive rages were far more frequent if he had been drinking in the evenings. With each drink, I could feel the tension in me rising as I knew that anything could trigger an outburst after he'd been drinking. He appeared to be out of control and volatile due to the drink, which meant I was more fearful.

In retrospect, I see that it was to make me less likely to speak out and confront him on his actions when he was drunk. If I

[5] Gilchrist ET al, 2003

challenged him about his behaviour when he was sober, he would inevitably blame the alcohol and promise to reduce the amount he drank.

Even after going to Alcoholics Anonymous, and stating that he was able to control his drinking and didn't need to completely quit, he continued to drink too much. The aggressive behaviour continued with the excuse that it was alcohol that caused his behaviour rather than it being down to him.

By blaming the alcohol, it meant that I wasn't looking at him but at the drink. My focus wasn't on his behaviour, but rather on the beers in the fridge. It deflected the issue from abuse to alcoholism. By shifting the focus and blame onto alcohol it also stopped Mark from taking any responsibility for his actions and stopped me holding him to account. "I'm sorry. I had no idea what I was doing last night. It was the drink. I promise I won't drink that much again."

Rather than holding him responsible, I tried to support him. I believed that it wasn't him — after all, he could be so loving and caring towards me and the children — so it must be this outside cause. By believing that it was the alcohol causing the abuse, I could also believe that it could be solved by removing the alcohol and getting Mark 'cured'. It meant that I could believe that Mark didn't mean it and that he must love me. Therefore, if I stayed and supported him through his alcohol problem, which I felt was part of my commitment to our marriage, then Mark would be better and we could have a happy marriage again.

I attempted to help cure him by encouraging him to cut down, doing the shopping myself (so he wouldn't be tempted to buy any) and persuading him to go to Alcoholics Anonymous. Not surprisingly, none of this worked because Mark didn't want to stop. Drinking not only provided him with what he thought was a valid excuse, but also got him some sympathy and support.

When a partner blames alcohol for their behaviour, rather than taking responsibility for it themselves, it shifts the focus away from what they are doing in the relationship and provides a problem that needs to be dealt with. The other partner wants to support him through this to get him better so that he will no longer be aggressive. On the other hand, he doesn't want to get rid of his excuse and take responsibility. Thus, it becomes an ongoing cycle of broken promises and frustration that nothing changes.

Also, when faced with a physically larger person who appears drunk, most people won't provoke a reaction. However, this gives the drunk partner the power as they know that when they are drinking, their partner will be submissive. Alcohol becomes a tool of power and control.

It may seem strange that a partner will believe that it is the alcohol rather than her partner who is at fault. However, this acceptance that it is the alcohol to blame means that her partner doesn't really mean to hurt her. If she accepts that it isn't the alcohol, then she is left with the fact that her partner is intentionally hurting her and this is a difficult realisation to come to.

Also, by blaming alcohol, it means that there is a solution — he can stop drinking and return to the person she used to know at the start of their relationship. By providing support, understanding and patience to the partner, the abuse can stop which gives her some control over the situation when she feels that she has none.

Just tackling the alcohol issue won't stop a partner being abusive. It may reduce the abuse for a time (particularly if he is physically abusive when drunk)[6] but reducing it is not the same as stopping it. Also, emotional and verbal abuse is likely to still occur whether he is drunk or sober. Both the alcohol and domestic abuse need to be recognised and addressed separately if there is to be a change. If only the alcohol abuse is resolved, the domestic abuse will continue, simply with a sober partner rather than a drunk one.

The only one who is responsible for their actions is the abusive partner. It is not the alcohol. The alcohol is an excuse at best, or a manipulative tool at worst, that is allowing the abuse to continue.

---

[6]   O'Farrell et al. 1999, 2003, 2004)

9
MENTAL ILLNESS

It is possible that your partner has a mental illness, so firstly, what is a mental illness? "If a person has *always* had a problem in their thinking, feeling or behaviour, then this is not usually called mental illness.   It may then be called a developmental problem or a difficulty with their personality (sometimes called a personality disorder)."[7]

Mental illness can include depression, post-traumatic stress disorder, anxiety, eating disorders, bipolar disorder, obsessive compulsive disorder and psychosis.

In cases when mental illness is contributing to the abuse of a partner, there will also be abusive behaviour to others, such as work colleagues, family or friends. If this is not happening, then it shows that he can control his words and actions in the company of some people and is reserving the hurtful actions for when he is with his partner. If he is able to have the awareness to make these choices, then mental illness is not the cause of his behaviour. He is in control and his words and actions towards his partner are intentional rather than being a result of a mental illness that is out

---

[7]   ISPS: International Society for Psychological and Social

Approaches to Psychology, http://ispsuk.org/?p=312, 2012

of his control.

He may choose to blame a mental illness, in a similar way that some abusers choose to blame their past trauma, alcohol or drugs, but it is simply shifting the responsibility from himself onto an illness to gain sympathy and support.

Even if a partner has a mental illness that effects their actions (no matter who they are with), it is not an excuse for abuse. They need to access professional help for both their mental illness and their behaviour to their partner.

Personality Disorders

There are a range of personality disorders but two types have been particularly linked to domestic abuse - Borderline Personality Disorder (BPD) and Narcissistic Personality Disorder (NPD).

Borderline Personality Disorder is best understood as a disorder of mood and how a person interacts with others.[8] It can cause intense, negative emotions with sudden mood swings (that are sometimes aggressive or violent), upsetting thought patterns, an unstable self-image and impulsive behaviour. They may fear abandonment, have paranoia, feel empty inside or use alcohol and/or drugs. This is just a brief overview and should not be used to diagnose a partner.

Those who have BPD have difficulties in relationships due to their behaviours and emotional instability. Some of the behaviours that they exhibit are emotionally abusive (even though they may not be intentional).

When a person with BPD feels negative about himself, he may use projection (as discussed in 'Using Your Emotions') to blame his partner for those feelings instead of himself. He will often deny having flaws or problems as that would mean accepting he is not perfect. Projection is a method that enables him to shift these

---

[8] www.nhs.co.uk

flaws onto his partner. This can result in confusion and a loss in self-confidence for the partner as she tries to make sense of the accusations and thought processes of her partner.

Constant blame and criticism are two other behavioural characteristics of someone with BPD that can cause hurt in his partner. Being criticised continually leads to her doubting her own ability or who she really is. It may be that the partner with BPD actually feels that it is him that has the fault, but rather than being able to admit his own faults, he will criticise his partner instead. Being attacked through criticism and blame leaves his partner feeling confused, rejected and destroys intimacy in the relationship.

When one partner in a relationship has BPD, it is not unusual for the other to feel as though she is in a partnership with someone who is inconsistent and contradictory. It may seem that he says one thing and then the total opposite moments later, leaving the partner trying to work out whether her memory is playing tricks on her or if she is going crazy. She may feel as though she can't communicate with her partner as it results in frustration and confusion.

While these behaviours aren't intentional, they all have the potential to hurt the non-BPD partner and can make it very difficult to maintain a relationship.

Narcissistic Personality Disorder

Narcissistic Personality Disorder is thought to effect 1% of the population, yet it isn't frequently diagnosed because those who may have it won't accept that there is a problem to ask for help. One of the traits is an exaggerated sense of superiority and distorted self-image, which is why they believe there is nothing wrong with them. Instead the problems lie with others around them.

Those with NPD may exaggerate their achievements and talents, be preoccupied by fantasies of their success and power, require excessive admiration, have a sense of entitlement, lack empathy, be envious of others and take advantage of others for their own gain.

Narcissists are manipulators. They need to control and have power over others as they have a fragile self-esteem. This fragility is hidden by arrogance and egotism. If they feel that they are being criticised, or things are not going the way they want them to, they feel anger which builds to a rage and aggression. They hold onto negative emotions such as resentment, letting them fester inside and bringing up the past at any opportunity. They never question themselves because they think they are always right. They won't accept responsibility for their actions or behaviour but will blame everything and everyone else. They are well practised liars. They expect their needs to be met and feel entitled to anything they want.

A woman who falls for a narcissist is often a care giver who wants to help the insecure child within her partner. She wants to give him enough love and care that he will get better. She may feel totally responsible for the both of them, always meeting his needs to make their relationship better. Yet, no matter what she tries, nothing seems to work and she can't put a finger on why. This confusion is further added to by feeling as though she is living with two different people — one who is loving, caring and attentive and the other who is critical, angry and unpredictable.

Someone with NPD can abuse his partner in a number of ways without having any recognition of their partner's feelings or the hurt that they are causing.

At the start of the relationship, he is highly likely to lavish his new partner with attention and love. He may make her feel special, wanting to spend lots of time with her, being protective, writing love letters and telling her that she is unlike anyone else he has dated.

However, over time, the focus of the relationship will shift so that it is centred around him. If she is enjoying herself, or the attention is on her, he can get jealous and seek to ruin her good mood and to bring the focus onto himself and his needs. The way in which he can do this is often through verbal and emotional abuse. For example, projection to move his faults onto her, or the silent treatment as a means of having power and control.

As someone with NPD is unable to take responsibility, he has to shift the blame onto others, which is often his partner. In his eyes he is never at fault and has no faults. If something goes wrong, he will blame others rather than accept responsibility. It could be alcohol, his childhood, work, his children or his partner that is responsible for his actions. If she accepts the excuses or the blame, she gives him permission to repeat the behaviour and continue to refuse to take responsibility.

Lying seems to be second nature for a narcissistic. He will lie about anything, often for no reason at all. It can be small lies such as whether he has put petrol in the car or paid a bill. Even though he knows that he will be caught out, it doesn't matter — he will just concoct a story to try and fit the new facts, all the time adding to the chaos. Often he will mix in half truths so the stories seem believable. Once a small part of the truth is believed, the story can be exaggerated and grown.

Sometimes the stories may be to make it appear that he has a more exciting/interesting life than he really does. For example, being a war hero, saving someone's life, having an illness or disorder, or escaping from some danger in the past. These lies tend to be to create drama and gain attention, but it also hides who he really is. A partner may fall in love with the character that is being portrayed in these stories, and if the truth does come out at a later date, then she may be left wondering who she has been having a relationship with. Once lies are exposed, the whole relationship can feel as though it was a sham, leaving her feeling as though she can't trust others or her own instincts.

It is his sense of entitlement that means he will do whatever he needs to (including abuse) to have what he wants, which is power and control. This will often mean that someone with NPD will abuse his partner by draining them emotionally and financially, leaving behind broken hearts and empty wallets. Financially, he may steal from his partner, run up debts and spend irresponsibly. He may feel that he is entitled to a range of benefits, promotions at work and his partner's savings. If he sees others with more wealth, he will be very envious and overtly critical of them.

A narcissist keeps control of his partner by keeping her off-balance and making her feel as though she is walking on eggshells. Just when she feels she knows how he will behave, he will change. For example, if he regularly shouts at his partner for not putting her shoes correctly on the rack, but doesn't one day, she will be left feeling uneasy at this unexpected change and apprehensive about when he will shout at her. Keeping her scared and on tenterhooks is part of the control that he desires. This provides him with the power and superiority in the relationship.

Someone with NPD may further use a mixture of techniques to confuse his partner to make her feel as though she is going crazy. He may use flattery, praise and lots of attention to make her feel special one day and the next, he may be critical, aloof or giving her the silent treatment. He may even say she's the only one who understands him and can make him better so that she feels she can't abandon him. If he then escalates this to saying that he can't live without her and will self-harm or commit suicide if she leaves, she feels totally responsible for his well-being and therefore trapped. Again, this is abusive and part of his desire to control her and have the dominance he feels he is entitled to.

One of the basic human rights he takes away from her is the right to be angry with him. No matter how badly he treats her, he believes that her voice shouldn't rise and she shouldn't be angry. The entitlement of rage is reserved for him alone. When she does show her anger, he is likely to use it against her to prove what an irrational person she is.

There isn't a cure for NPD and those who agree to go to therapy will often use it to be able to portray themselves as a victim and blame others. Therapy can provide a place for them to have the attention they crave, rather than get better.

The non-NPD partner will often feel as though she is going crazy. Conversations don't make sense, she questions her memory, she can't make him happy, he seems to change on a daily basis with no explanation, she's apologising and she doesn't know why, and she feels tense and anxious for no reason. Her self-esteem and confidence may have been destroyed, yet she still feels as though she needs to take care of him.

The relationship with a partner with Narcissistic Personality Disorder is complex, unhealthy and usually abusive.

SECTION 4 – EFFECTS OF AN ABUSIVE RELATIONSHIP

10
EFFECTS ON THE PARTNER

The effects of domestic abuse vary from person to person and so this chapter won't be exhaustive, but hopefully it will provide some understanding of the effects that this abuse creates.

Any type of abuse may have an effect on the physical and mental health of the person it's targeted at. With domestic abuse, 75% of cases result in physical injury or mental health consequences to women.[9]

This may happen during the relationship, but can sometimes take months or years to show itself. If a woman's mental health is affected during the relationship, it won't disappear when she leaves the relationship. The impact of domestic abuse can be seen for months and years after the end of an abusive relationship.

Shockingly between 50% and 60% of female users of mental health services have experienced domestic violence, and up to 20% will

---

[9] Home Office, 2001

currently be experiencing abuse[10], which shows abuse still affects women even after it stops.

My relationship with Mark left me with both physical and mental health problems. My depression was diagnosed towards the end of our relationship, but my physical symptoms didn't show themselves until two years afterwards. I knew there was something wrong for the two years leading up to my depression diagnosis, but like many women I didn't want to ask for help for fear of the professionals stepping in and saying that I couldn't cope. That didn't happen. In fact, my doctor was very supportive and listened to me. Health visitors and social services didn't get involved and my fears were unfounded.

When I spoke to the doctor I voiced that I felt I was going mad; that things didn't make sense in my life and it felt as though I was walking in a fog where I couldn't see where I was going or what was happening. I explained the constant butterflies in my stomach and not wanting to get up in the morning. Being diagnosed with depression made me feel as if I wasn't going mad — there was something wrong and I wasn't imagining it. Yet, the depression was a symptom of what was really wrong and nobody picked up on it (including myself). While I could take medication to help me feel better, it didn't remove the cause of the depression. The cause was being in a long-term, abusive relationship while I tried to keep my family together.

Like me, many women will suffer mental illness during their relationship, but often they won't seek help for mental health issues until after a long length of time, or after they have left the relationship. It may be that they don't feel they are able to ask for help while with their partner. He may have stopped her seeking help or she may know that he will then use it against her rather than supporting her. She may be afraid of the consequences of professionals stepping in, especially if there is children involved.

---

[10]   [(Department of Health, 2003; Bowstead, Janet, 2000;

ReSisters, 2002)]

Also, if she does see a doctor and gets diagnosed with a mental illness, her partner may accuse her of being mad, incapable of doing anything without him, or even threaten that she will lose the children due to her mental health if she leaves him. This leaves her feeling even more helpless and trapped, increasing her sense of isolation.

Depression and Anxiety

Depression and anxiety have been linked (by numerous studies) to domestic abuse, with depression the most common by-product of being in an abusive relationship. In fact, women in an abusive relationship are four times as likely to suffer from depression, compared to those not in an abusive relationship.[11] Being depressed can make a person feel low spirited, irritable, helpless, numb, empty, restless, guilty and isolated. These feelings are similar to, or even the same as, the feelings that are produced when a partner is abused by the other partner, so it can be difficult to tell whether it is the abuse, depression or a combination of the two causing the feelings. Also, as depression can lower self-esteem and self-worth, it makes it easier for a partner to abuse his partner if she has depression. So, being in an abusive relationship can cause depression, but depression can also lead to an increase of abuse in a relationship.

It is not surprising that those in an abusive relationship often have anxiety, as anxiety is linked to fear. Not knowing when her partner may change from Jekyll into Hyde, whether he is going to shout at her for not tidying the house, or whether he will blame her for something she hasn't done, can make her feel as though she's constantly on alert. This sense of impending danger produces physical symptoms such as a faster heart beat and/or breathing, feeling weakness in the body, knotted or churning stomach, sweating or having tense muscles. Mentally, it can cause a fuzzy head where it is hard to focus or concentrate, a nagging sense of something being wrong, or forgetfulness.

---

[11] World Health Organisaton

Anxiety can also lead to panic attacks, which is when there is a rapid build up of the body's normal response to fear. Someone having a panic attack may feel their heartbeat pounding, feel faint, have chest pains, feel shaky and not connected to their body. It can be a scary experience as it feels as though you have lost control of both your body and emotions.

This anxiety may not only be there when her partner is present. Due to being on heightened alert, other things that may seem 'normal' activities may trigger anxiety or a panic attack. She may also be anxious about other aspects of her life, such as whether to leave or not, fear of being judged by professionals, friends or family or worried about what the future holds.

This cycle and the feelings that depression and anxiety causes means that it is hard for someone in an abusive relationship to be able to see what is happening and to be able to leave the relationship. Instead of seeing that her partner is abusing her, she may see herself as having a mental illness which may increase her feelings of worthlessness, leaving her more vulnerable to abuse from her partner. She may even believe that she is the one to blame for her feelings and that she is a failure as a partner. She may even feel that if she wasn't ill, her partner would be happier and their relationship would be better. He may encourage these beliefs as it moves the focus and blame from his behaviour onto her. He can then play the victim in the relationship.

Alternatively, he may use her mental illness to dominate her by telling her that she is unable to do anything without him. He can reduce her self-esteem further by telling others that she is mad and gaining sympathy from them for having to care for her. He may become more controlling by not letting her go to places alone or speaking for her and justify this as being for her own good while she is not thinking straight. If she fights against his dominance he may threaten to have her sectioned, take away her medication or even contact social services to have the children taken away from her.

Often anxiety doesn't disappear when the relationship ends because it becomes an ingrained coping mechanism to stress. She may also suffer flashbacks and small everyday events may trigger a difficult memory, resulting in a heightening in anxiety. It is very hard to re-programme the brain to find other ways to cope with stress, but it is possible. Often a woman will need professional help with this. Cognitive Behavioural Therapy or hypnotherapy can be particularly useful, as well as having supportive friends and family.

Depression can stay for years after the end of an abusive relationship. In addition, the grief of losing a partner and a relationship can compound this depression. She has lost a partner, maybe a home, maybe friends and family during the relationship break-up and might be feeling the weight of building a new life.

While she has left an abusive relationship, initially, things are difficult on a practical and emotional level. It is easy to believe that a woman who has left an abusive relationship is suddenly happier, yet, the massive change in her life means that she needs support and care in this period of time.

It is in the early stages of a relationship ending that women may return to the abusive partner because trying to manage a new life can seem daunting, and she may feel that she is unable to do it by herself. This belief can often be because of the emotional and verbal abuse that she has had that has left her feeling as though she is not capable of being independent. If he has been putting her down and implying that she is nothing without him, then he will often be the first person that she asks for help when she is struggling in her new life alone.

Anti-depressants can help with depression, but counselling and therapy are also often necessary for a woman to be able to understand what was happening in the relationship, understand her own emotional responses and help her to be able to find herself again.

Post-Traumatic Stress Disorder

Post-Traumatic Stress Disorder (PTSD) is commonly thought of as a psychological disorder that soldiers get after serving in war zones. However, it is not uncommon for those in, or those who have left an abusive relationship, to also develop PTSD. The extent that PTSD will effect someone varies from person to person. Some may have it for a few months and others may have it for years. Some may have many of the symptoms and others less.

As PTSD can often develop after the end of an abusive relationship, as a result of the stress that she has lived with for years, the abused partner may feel as though she is still trapped there as she is still feeling the effects of the abuse. For example, she may see a man walking towards her, with the same stature and coat as her ex-partner, and her heart may start beating quickly, she may start sweating and she might feel lightheaded. Or if someone makes a sudden movement, she might automatically flinch. She may suffer from frequent nightmares in which she relives particularly distressing scenes from her relationship, or she may panic at the thought of being in crowded spaces or leaving her home.

There are many symptoms of PTSD and they can often overlap with depression and anxiety symptoms. A mental health specialist can diagnose whether the symptoms are PTSD, depression, anxiety or a combination. There is a range of treatment such as psychotherapy, CBT and medication. Hypnotherapy may also help.

Physical Injuries

If a partner is physically abusive, then there is a high possibility of an injury being sustained by the other partner. Injuries such as fractures, cuts, bruises, miscarriages and scars are possible and there may be long-term impacts of the injuries that have been caused.

Even when the abuse doesn't involves a physical assault, there can still be physical effects. For example, recurrent headaches, high blood pressure or gastrointestinal disorders due to living in a stressful environment. These may last for years after the end of the relationship and often aren't seen as being directly related to the abuse, as they don't present themselves as directly related injuries. Yet there is a higher occurrence of these conditions in women who have been abused than women who haven't.

There is also evidence that Chronic Fatigue Syndrome, Arthritis and Fibromyalgia can be triggered by traumatic events such as living with abuse and trying to cope with mental and emotional stress over a long period of time. It is believed that it could be due to the body releasing high levels of the stress hormone, cortisol, over a long period of time. Eventually that can take its toll on the body, leading to constant exhaustion or pain, as the body tries to cope with the brain's responses.[12] It's the biological impact of chronic stress caused by living with an abusive partner.

Emotional Health

The first emotion that I struggled with when we initially split up was guilt. I felt guilty for the children's sake; that I was depriving them of a parent and a secure, stable home. Mark emphasised this point to me over the early weeks, especially when our youngest baby was born only three weeks after he left. Mark managed to make me feel guilty for not being a family and told me that I wasn't being fair on the children by keeping them apart from him.

On the other hand, I felt guilty for not protecting the children enough. For letting them be in this situation where they had heard and witnessed Mark's anger towards me and towards them. The involvement of Social Services increased this burden of guilt. I was left feeling as though I had completely failed them as a mother because I hadn't protected them.

I also felt guilty towards Mark as, three days after he left the family home, he told me that he had been diagnosed with post-traumatic stress disorder, so I felt guilty for not taking him back to help him.

---

[12] http://dartcenter.org/content/hidden-cause-chronic-illness

This was further compounded when he was admitted into hospital or arrested for his drinking. Each time that he was in hospital or police custody, he would request that they contact me to let me know where he was and his condition. As throughout the rest of our relationship, I felt responsible for his welfare and his behaviour. It was when I told the woman from the domestic abuse unit about the phone calls from the hospital and police, that she explained he was still emotionally abusing me by manipulating me to make feel guilty and take him back. She contacted the custody unit and ensured that they wouldn't be telling me if he was arrested again.

Mark took it further then, drinking more and ending up in more dangerous situations, until two months after we broke up, he was put in intensive care after consuming enough alcohol to kill himself. The hospital phoned me at two o'clock in the morning and I instantly felt awful, knowing that if I hadn't made him leave, he wouldn't be in intensive care. I hoped and prayed that he would survive, just so that I wouldn't be carrying the weight of responsibility and guilt for his death for the rest of my life.

Over time the guilt reduced as I began to see that he was making his own decisions and I was not responsible for him or his actions. Actions that were often taken to hurt me or to try and persuade me to take him back.

Guilt is such a powerful emotion and one which can be used against the other partner as a form of manipulation.

During the relationship, one partner can make the other feel guilty for not being a good enough parent, for failing to fulfil the duties of a wife, for spending money on herself, for provoking him — in fact, for anything that he blames her for.

In addition, she may feel guilty for not protecting the children if they had heard or seen abuse, which will be further compounded if the children have also been abused by the partner.

If she leaves, she can still be made to feel guilty, either by her ex-partner or by her own belief that she is solely responsible for the relationship.

It can take time for the mentality that she is solely responsible for the welfare of everyone in the family and the resulting guilt to go. It takes a shift in thinking, and realising that her thought patterns are a result of long-term manipulation and persuasion. She shouldn't shoulder the blame for breaking up a family, the children being hurt or the actions that he may take as a result of the break-up. It takes time, and sometimes counselling or CBT is needed, but it is possible to move from a place of shouldering the blame and feeling guilty for particular situations, to being able to accept that he is largely responsible for the events and the consequences. He may never accept that responsibility but, in her own mind, she can take it off herself and place it with him.

With domestic abuse there is often shame and embarrassment. I know that I didn't tell anyone about most of Mark's actions while we were together. I told friends about arguments, and they would tell me about the arguments that they had with their partners, which made everything seem quite normal. Just the typical arguments that all partners have. I didn't tell them about him smashing things up, puffing out his chest, clenching his fists while looming over me, threatening suicide or the effects that his behaviour was having on me. I was too embarrassed because, deep down, I knew that it wasn't normal, no matter how many times I told myself and rationalised with myself that it was. The fact that I held things back through shame of people finding out, shows that I did know it was abuse, even if I wasn't ready to admit it to myself, let alone anyone else.

It can be humiliating for someone to admit that they are being abused. To say that someone has power and control over you is a difficult thing to acknowledge. If a woman is independent, strong, professional and assured in the rest of her life, it is particularly hard and embarrassing to tell others that they are being dominated in their own home.

Embarrassment can keep some women in the relationship but it can also affect them after the relationship has ended. They may not wish to tell others about why the relationship ended and would rather take the blame instead of telling the truth because they are too embarrassed about it.

Being in an abusive relationship can result in finding it hard to trust others. A woman may feel that if she believes and trusts someone who seems to care for her, that she might end up being hurt again. This may be more the case if the abusive partner was a Jekyll and Hyde character as she will know that some people aren't who they appear to be and can pretend to be someone else.

That lack of trust can stop her being able to confide in friends, meet new friends or have other romantic relationships. Without close relationships, loneliness and a sense of isolation can occur which may lead to depression. It is important to learn to trust again, but understandably (when someone has been lied to, manipulated and dominated for years), it is also difficult to do.

Anger is also an understandable emotional response to being in an abusive relationship. She may feel angry towards him and his behaviour — for his aggression, his lies, the names he called her, his heavy drinking or the debts that he ran up. She may feel angry for the impact that his behaviour has had on her and her life — physically, mentally and emotionally.

She may also feel angry towards herself. Possibly angry that she allowed it to go on for so long, or that she didn't do anything to stop it earlier. She may feel angry that she believed his lies and feel that she was weak for letting him have power over her.

However, someone who has been in an abusive relationship is not weak and has done nothing wrong. She is likely to have used every bit of her strength to try and make her relationship work, despite her partner hurting her and making the relationship unworkable.

Another emotion that I felt, and so do many others, is confusion. This will often start during the relationship, as causing confusion, or making her feel as though she is going crazy, is part of emotional abuse. She may be confused about who she is married to and try to work out who he really is — the caring sensitive man or the angry liar? Or, she might wonder why he is saying or doing the things to her when he can see the hurt it causes. She may be trying to work out if he really loves her, or even if love should hurt like it does for her. There is also confusion over what is the truth and what are lies.

Even now, years after the end of my marriage, I am still confused by a lot of it. I don't know what he spent thousands on that got us in debt. I have spent time trying to work out who I was really married to — what was really Mark and what was just an act to gain power and control? I have also examined things he used to say to try and find out what part was the truth and what wasn't.

Unfortunately, I have not found the answers, which is why I am still confused. However, I don't let the emotion of confusion have a significant impact on my life any more.

Confusion over words and actions are common because so little of it seems to make logical sense, no matter how many times it is examined. The confusion that results from an abusive relationship can be damaging because it can lead her to doubt herself and her own intuition and thoughts. This is what the other partner wants though — someone who doesn't know what is going on, who is living in a fog of confusion so that they are easier to manipulate and dominate.

This is also why it is important to move from a state of confusion to knowledge and understanding. By recognising the abusive behaviour and having the knowledge that she was only confused because her partner's words and actions caused her to be, it is possible to leave the confusion behind and grow in confidence.

As there are effects on both the mind and body of a partner in an abusive relationship, it seems obvious to state that she should leave as early as possible in order to limit the short-term and long-term effects on herself. Yet, as the chapter To Leave or Stay discusses, this is not as easy as it sounds, which is why the damage to a woman's mental, emotional and physical health may be so high.

11
EFFECTS ON THE CHILDREN

My children have been affected by my relationship with Mark even though, at the time, I didn't think they were being. In the early years I thought that Mark's anger wasn't impacted on them because it was happening in the evenings when they were in bed. I thought that it was just affecting me. So, I persevered in the relationship, wanting that stable family life that I envisioned for my children. Thinking that if I worked harder at it, supported him more, we could have that idealistic family life.

Hindsight is a wonderful thing. Now I know that I should have ended the relationship earlier. Rather than staying together to try and provide a secure environment for our children, it would have been a more secure environment if I had left.

In the three years that Mark and I have been apart there has been many challenges, but the children have been happier and never said to me that they wished he was still living with us. In fact, quite the opposite; they wish that I had done it earlier. Looking back, so do I.

While my older children say that they didn't notice it as much when they were younger, it was still there. They do remember particular incidents — holidays, birthdays and Christmases tainted by Mark's words or temper. They would have picked up on the tension in the room when he came home from work. They would have sensed my frustration and confusion at trying to communicate with him.

At an older age they remember Mark's behaviour very clearly because they were also a target of it.

While I worked two evenings a week, he would call them names, smash things, hit walls, scream and shout. They didn't tell me until the relationship was over. The guilt that I felt, knowing that they couldn't tell me, was crippling. I felt that I had failed as a parent and that my decision to keep trying to repair our relationship was the worst mistake that I had made. The abuse impacting on me was one thing, but when I realised it had impacted on our children, it wracked me with anger and regret.

Mark used some of the same abusive tactics with the older children that he had with me. For example, he would change from being kind and caring to being aggressive and shouting within minutes to keep them on edge. He asked them to keep secrets from me, particularly about his behaviour and drinking while I wasn't there, and used to buy them small treats and gifts to persuade them not to tell me. He would call them names such as pig, selfish cow and lazy. The effect of those words and actions is still being felt today.

As I explained earlier, one of my daughters started to experience long fainting spells at a difficult point in mine and Mark's relationship. Over the years, there were numerous tests and theories, from a heart condition to low sugar levels. As time went on, the faints became more like seizures and she was referred to a neurologist with suspected epilepsy. It took another 18 months before she was finally diagnosed with non-epileptic attacks — a condition brought on by traumatic events that will often continue in times of stress or anxiety.

The domestic abuse at home was directly related to my daughter's non-epileptic attacks. It was her way of coping with her father's volatile and unpredictable behaviour. It wasn't a conscious choice, but the only way that her brain could manage — by shutting off from the world completely. The non-epileptic attacks didn't stop when our relationship ended. It took years of trying different therapies such as counselling, CBT and hypnotherapy, and various practitioners before a turning point arrived.

My older daughter suffered from nightmares, panic attacks and anxiety as a direct result from seeing and hearing her father shouting, screaming and smashing things up. She had some counselling under CAHMS (Child and Adolescent Mental Health Services) and then, after our move she saw a private counsellor who helped her work through her memories and gave her practical ways to manage her anxiety. Her counsellor has said that she strongly suspects that my daughter has Post-Traumatic Stress Disorder from living in a house where there was an abusive relationship.

Knowing that they have been affected to such an extent — both physically and mentally — is a constant reminder that I should have left the relationship earlier. Yet, I held onto the dream of having that loving family life. And, because Mark could be a caring, considerate father at times, I felt that there was hope of this dream coming true. Now I know differently.

It is not just *my* children that have been affected by domestic abuse. Research that children witness about three-quarters of the abusive incidents[13]. This means that there are hundreds of thousands of other children who are being affected.

As children are affected by witnessing domestic abuse, it becomes child abuse. And even if they don't witness the abuse directly, they may hear it or pick up on the tension in the house. If the mother's mental health is negatively affected by her partner's abuse, then this will also impact on the children. The hard truth is that even when mothers feel that they are protecting their children from their partner's abuse, the chances are that their children are or will be affected.

This may exhibit itself in different ways. In my children, it showed

---

[13] Royal College of Psychiatrists (2004)

as panic attacks and non-epileptic attacks. In younger children it may be exhibited through stomach aches, bed-wetting, having trouble going to sleep, temper tantrums, being overly attached to the non-abusive parent, being aggressive to other children, or having speech delays. Obviously these symptoms can have other explanations other than being in an abusive home. However there are clear links between being bought up in a house where there is domestic abuse and having developmental issues.[14]

Older children can have problems at school and may get behind or play truant. Boys may use physical aggression or violence to deal with the issues at home, whereas girls may become withdrawn and self-harm through cutting themselves, or develop an eating disorder to try and gain some control of a situation where they have none.

Like the adult who is suffering abuse, children can feel depressed and anxious as they try to deal with the uncertainty and unpredictability of home life. This can last after the abusive relationship has ended.

The long-term effects of living in a home where there is an abusive relationship can be low self-esteem, feelings of unworthiness and isolation, which could result in them being vulnerable to abuse themselves in the future. There may be flashbacks, nightmares and physical symptoms of post-traumatic stress disorder. Some may turn to alcohol or drugs to try and stop negative feelings and thoughts. It can also negatively impact on their education as they may find it hard to concentrate at school which further impacts on their future prospects.

There is a clear link in various studies between domestic abuse and child abuse. If an adult abuses his partner, he is more likely to abuse his children than a parent who doesn't abuse his partner. In fact, a third of children witnessing domestic violence also experienced another form of abuse.[15]

---

[14] 4 Osofsky, Joy D., 'The Impact of Violence on Children'

[15] Radford, L. et al

Like me, a parent may be unaware of what is going on but that doesn't mean that it isn't happening. The children in an abusive relationship are at risk of being abused — physically, mentally and emotionally. The potential for long-term damage to a child who is being made to feel worthless, unloved and scared is very high.

As with partner-to-partner abuse, there are many ways in which a parent can abuse a child and most are the same or similar.

Physically, a parent can use their hands or household implements to hurt their child. They may often call it discipline but it will go beyond the tap on the hand or the bottom that other parents may give. A parent may also use their physical size to intimidate a child by shouting in their face, having an aggressive stance to make their child fearful or throw household items around in anger.

Emotional abuse is not as straightforward to recognise, yet is suspected to be the second most common type of abuse after neglect (although there are links between the two).

Verbally putting a child down, name calling or belittling their needs is one form that emotional abuse may take. Telling a child that they are ugly, fat, stupid or that they wish they would leave can cause a child to grow up believing that they are worthless. The criticisms and insults may be camouflaged as jokes, but they will have the same impact on the child. If it is demeaning and reduces the child's self-esteem, then it is abusive.

A parent may target one child of the family and make them the family scapegoat, ridiculing them in front of their siblings or blaming them for problems in the house. They may also exclude them from family activities which causes them to feel isolated and unable to talk to the other parent or their siblings.

Refusing to talk to a child as a form of punishment or withholding physical contact can also be considered abuse. Failing to respond to a child, being emotionally unavailable or not interacting with a child can result in the child not being able to socially interact with others or being emotionally responsive.

A parent may threaten a child with harsh words, physical harm, severe consequences, leaving home themselves or kicking the child out. They may also threaten to harm a pet, favourite object or another member of the family if they don't comply. Threats place the responsibility for the actions of the parent on the child. This controls the child and makes them fearful of what may or may not happen.

The abusive parent may reward or encourage behaviour that is inappropriate, such as violence, lying and stealing. Or they may reward secrecy by bribing their child not to speak out about the parent's behaviour or actions, placing the child in a difficult position. Encouraging a child to drink, smoke or take drugs, and supplying the means to do so, is also a form of child abuse as the child will try to please the parent who is acting illegally.

No parent who is being abused themselves will want their child to be suffering in the same way. However, too often they don't see it. Either because they can't see that they are being abused themselves, or because the abusive parent puts up barriers so that she can't see the truth. For example, telling the children to keep it a secret, doing it when the other parent isn't present or manipulating the family so that there is no open communication.

The desire to have a strong family unit, the belief that she can make him better, the manipulation and her own mental health can mean that a parent doesn't see what domestic abuse is doing to her children. For the sake of children in these situations, it is crucial that abuse is recognised for what it is and support given to break free.

My children still have some long-term effects from my marriage but, without the presence of a partner who manipulates and lies, they are improving. I wish that I had seen it earlier — both my own situation and my children's — and I hope that other parents will see what is happening in their relationship before it negatively impacts on their children. Desiring a strong loving family unit is a positive dream for our children but it doesn't need two parents to achieve this.

A child is better to have one loving parent rather than two parents of whom one is abusive to the other.

SECTION 5 – WILL HE EVER CHANGE?

12
WILL HE EVER CHANGE?

One of the reasons that I stayed in my marriage for so long was because I believed that Mark could, and would, change back to the person I first met if I gave him enough support and love.

He would say sorry and beg forgiveness for shouting or smashing something up. He would promise that he would change. And he often would, for a short period of time. Enough time to remind me that he could be kind and caring, before slipping back into the aggressive and unpredictable Mark.

During the more difficult periods of our marriage I used to sit down and consider my situation.

Maybe I was under stress and so being melodramatic.

Maybe Mark was under stress and needed a supportive wife rather than one who was considering leaving. (This thought always made me feel guilty for even considering it).

Maybe it would get better — just a bad phase like everyone has in their relationship.

Maybe it's not that bad. After all, there's far worse stories in the newspapers — my relationship seems positive compared to others.

What about the impact on the children? I wouldn't want them to lose a stable home while they're young and vulnerable.

If I just put in a bit more effort, Mark wouldn't be so angry and he would be like the old Mark at the beginning of our relationship.

Maybe if I could help Mark be less stressed or deal with his issues. Then he would be happier and our relationship would be better.

It took many people, including professionals, to finally open my eyes to what was happening. Mark was playing a game in which he would use his body and words to hurt me until I felt low and confused, at which point he would say that he was sorry and promise to change. A promise that he didn't keep.

A lot of women feel the same — they want to fight for their marriage and they want to help their partner. He may seem to be emotionally needy and so her caring side will continually try to fix him and make him better. However, meeting his needs won't solve the problem. She ends up trying various things, from being more caring towards him and giving him what he asks for, to arranging counselling for him. Yet, he still criticises her, makes her feel guilty and continues to be a Jekyll and Hyde character. No matter what she gives him, or what she does, it isn't enough because he believes that he is entitled to all that and more.

If he doesn't have respect for his partner and always puts his needs first, they will never have a balanced relationship in which they can share things without her fearing potential consequences.

Generally I'm a big advocate for giving people second chances (unless there is physical or sexual violence involved). Everyone, including myself, makes genuine mistakes. But when a person repeats the mistake time and time again, it no longer appears to be a mistake but an intentional action.

It is possible for people to change. However, they have to want it and agree to get help to enable them to change. This is where the problem often lies. The partner being hurt can see that there is a problem, but often the abusive partner can't. He enjoys the power and control in the relationship and to change would mean giving that up and having an equal relationship with his partner instead. It would mean not only a change in himself, but also a change in his belief systems and the relationship. It's not impossible to change but it can be difficult and take time.

If he does want to change he must take responsibility for his past actions, his present behaviour and his future behaviour. He can no longer blame alcohol, his past, stress at work or anything else. He can't say, "I accept responsibility and know that it is all my fault, but…". When he stops shifting the blame, he accepts that he was the only one in charge of his actions and he is the only one who can stop it happening again.

That means that she must accept that she can't make him better or fix him (even though they may both wish that to happen or see their roles in that manner). Instead, it has to be his choice to change and he needs to accept that his past actions were solely his choice. If he tells his partner, "I can't change unless you do", he is not taking responsibility and still expects her to do something in exchange.

He will also need to realise that their relationship will change to one in which he is no longer dominant. Moving from a relationship in which he has control to one in which they are equal takes some adjustments. This adjustment will involve respecting her independence and choices without criticism or consequences. She is her own person and should be respected as such.

It is more difficult to change when someone has a personality disorder and, if it is possible, they will need a lot of professional support.

It may be that there needs to be a separation so that both partners can take a step back and evaluate what the issues were in their relationship, and how they feel without the influence of the other partner. If there is physical or sexual violence then a physical separation is very likely needed for the partner's own safety.

If he does seek help and says that he wants to change, it is important that she knows whether he is just saying and doing the right things to stay in the relationship and to continue to be abusive, or whether he really is going to change. Unfortunately, saying the right words, or attending therapy, isn't proof that things will be different. Some will pretend that things will be different but then go back to their old ways over time — slowly so that she doesn't notice at first until she feels trapped and exhausted again.

Professional programmes and therapies will be necessary to facilitate the change. Refusing to get help, criticising programmes, saying that he can do it by himself or just with her support, shows that he isn't ready to change. He isn't prepared for anyone to see what is really going on in the relationship or see him as he really is. Without professional help it is highly likely that he will temporarily change his ways, lulling her into a false sense of security, before continuing them once more. This cycle will carry on indefinitely while she is the caregiver and he is the abuser who refuses help.

Another sign that he may not be willing to change is by continuing to trivialise the abuse or even deny it. If he's saying things like "I never hit you" or "You were just as bad", he isn't accepting responsibility and is instead defending his behaviour. He may even pass the blame onto his partner by telling her that she made him do things that he didn't want to do.

He may apologise profusely, yet underlying the apology is the thinking that he isn't sorry for the action, but the consequences of the action. For example, "I'm sorry that we are having to have marriage counselling" or "I'm sorry that things are bad right now and that I have to cut down on my drinking".

He may even say sorry but continue to blame others; "I'm sorry for being a terrible husband and I know that I need help for how my mum treated me because I'm still hurting". Again, this isn't accepting responsibility but shifting it to someone else and also focusing on his hurt rather than his partner's. It is a sign that he may not change his behaviour.

If she tries to explain that she is hurt he may react angrily or continue to bring the focus back to his hurt and his problems, refusing to see that she has been negatively affected by his behaviour. He doesn't appear to understand why she was upset, fearful or confused by his actions and words. He doesn't understand why she struggles to trust him or believe his promises when he has broken them in the past. Without understanding how he has affected others, he won't be able to change his behaviour and stop hurting his partner in the future.

Instead of taking the initiative to go to therapy, alcohol treatment programmes or to get external support, he may rely on his partner to organise this for him, showing again that he doesn't really want to change. Likewise, he may say that he can only change if she provides support and understanding of his position, placing the onus on her. If they are separated he may use manipulation to move back in by explaining that he can't change while he is living alone because he is too unhappy, stating that he needs to move back in to stop drinking and be a better partner. He may even say things like, "I've changed but how can I show you if you won't let me move back in?" All of these tactics place her in the position of being the one responsible for him changing. If he doesn't change then he will blame her for not supporting him or not taking him back in to the home.

Change is possible but it needs the abusive partner to accept that he alone is to blame and he alone is the one that has to change.

It is often hard to accept that nothing that the partner can do will change him. No amount of love, attention, acceptance, arguing, persuasion, gifts or anything else that she can do will change the abusive behaviour.

SECTION 6 – CHRISTIAN RELATIONSHIPS

13
ABUSE IN CHRISTIAN RELATIONSHIPS

My ex-husband and I claim to be Christians, so how could our marriage be abusive? Unfortunately, being in a Christian marriage doesn't stop it being an abusive marriage. Abuse doesn't discriminate and is found in marriages of all religions, of all races and at all ages.

As a Christian, I had the belief that marriage was a lifetime commitment and God condemned divorce. Whatever problems we encountered in our relationship, it was possible to overcome them with love for each other, following the Bible and forgiveness. I thought that being in a relationship with someone else who claimed to be a Christian would mean that we would have a relationship built on love and respect.

As I have explained previously, it took having the situation and my marriage taken out of my control and being put into the hands of professional before I could see the truth. The truth that I was in an abusive relationship.

It didn't matter what religion either of us were, what our jobs were or how things appeared on the outside — abuse still happened in our marriage. Those who proclaim to be Christians aren't exempt from abusing others. Those in power in the Church with responsible roles aren't exempt from abusing others. Being in a relationship with someone who says that he is a Christian, goes to Church or has a leadership role in the Church, doesn't mean that the relationship isn't abusive — it can be and it does happen.

Whether I would have seen the abuse in my marriage earlier if I didn't have my Christian beliefs I don't know, but I do know that I felt under pressure to make my marriage succeed as I felt that divorce was against the Church's teachings. Instead, I saw marriage as part of a journey with ups and downs, but ultimately a journey of two people who were in love and prepared to make it work. Even walking into my local Christian bookshop I was presented with books on marriage advice and how to fix relationships. There wasn't a single book that seemed to accept that sometimes marriage vows have to be broken for the safety and welfare of those involved.

Since my marriage has ended, my thinking has changed, and my relationship with God is stronger. For those who are Christians, or helping a Christian, I hope to be able to lift the fog on Christian abusive relationships.

At the most difficult times in our marriage, and when I felt at my lowest, I read books and searched the internet for solutions. There were lots of stories from those who had overcome great adversity and problems in their relationships and had come through the other side stronger. I held onto the hope that it would happen for Mark and I if I followed their suggestions. These ranged from praying daily for my husband and praising God for bringing Mark into my life, to focusing more on his needs and thanking him more often to make him happier and feel more worthy. Nothing mentioned the word abuse or that it could happen in a Christian marriage. I continued trying to improve my marriage without being aware of what was really going on.

Without recognition that the relationship is abusive, nothing changes and the abuse continues. Meanwhile, the wife feels as though she is slowly going mad and feels worthless and empty.

God designed us to be in intimate relationships with each other as it explains in Genesis:

"The Lord God said, "It is not good for the man to be alone. I will make a helper suitable for him."

Now the Lord God had formed out of the ground all the wild animals and all the birds in the sky. He brought them to the man to see what he would name them; and whatever the man called each living creature, that was its name. So the man gave names to all the livestock, the birds in the sky and all the wild animals.

But for Adam no suitable helper was found. So the Lord God caused the man to fall into a deep sleep; and while he was sleeping, he took one of the man's ribs and then closed up the place with flesh. Then the Lord God made a woman from the rib he had taken out of the man, and he brought her to the man.

The man said,
"This is now bone of my bones
  and flesh of my flesh;
she shall be called 'woman,'
  for she was taken out of man."

That is why a man leaves his father and mother and is united to his wife, and they become one flesh." (Genesis 2:18-24 NIV).

These verses show that God approves of marriage and views that men and women need a partner to make them happy and to grow. The relationship is there to support each other and God recognises that as humans, we need close relationships to stop us being lonely.

What is sometimes a point of discussion are the verses that state Adam was made first and then Eve was made from him, followed by Eve being called Adam's helper. Some believe that this means that Eve is subservient or lesser than Adam, as Adam was first and therefore is the leader in the relationship, with Eve being a helper to aid him. In an abusive relationship the abuser may use scripture, such as these verses in Genesis, as evidence that he should be the one in the relationship with the control and power.

However, it could also be argued that God delayed the creation of Eve to make it clear to us that we are created for one another. Humans need each other, and most humans have need of a spouse. By forming Eve from Adam, it is not showing that she was lesser than him but that she is from him and therefore equal to him. Eve can't be beneath Adam when she is created from him, just as one part of a body is no lesser than another part. They are from the same flesh and so they are equal counterparts.

I don't believe to be called Adam's helper is a term suggestive of submission. To be able to help another person you need strength, wisdom, knowledge and empathy. Being a helper isn't a submissive role but one of responsibility and strength. Those who are weak can't help others. Eve wasn't Adam's servant or inferior to him. Instead, she was there to support him and aid him, in the same way that wives today will support and aid their partners because they love them.

It is also important to notice that God himself is called 'Helper' throughout the Old Testament:

"My father's God was my helper." (NIV, Exodus 18:4)

"You [God] are the helper of the fatherless." (NIV, Psalm 10:14)

"The Lord is with me; he is my helper." (NIV, Psalm 118:7)

The term 'helper' is therefore not a submissive term but a positive acknowledgement of God's ability and compassion to help us. Similarly, women have the ability and compassion to help her partner. Being named as 'Helper' is not a term to imply weakness but strength. Women are not lesser than men and using the Bible to suggest that men should be dominant and controlling to justify abuse is simply wrong.

In Genesis 2:24-25 Moses explains that as Eve was created from Adam, they are two halves of a whole, and when they join together in marriage they become one flesh. When a man and a woman join together they recognise in each other a part of themselves that was missing and they feel incomplete without each other. By becoming one flesh they are complete and God is telling us that by marrying another, we find completion and happiness.

The phrase "they become one flesh" is often used when discussing divorce. In Matthew's Gospel, divorce is discussed when Jesus is asked about this issue:

"Haven't you read," he replied, "that at the beginning the Creator 'made them male and female,' and said, 'For this reason a man will leave his father and mother and be united to his wife, and the two will become one flesh'? So they are no longer two, but one flesh. Therefore what God has joined together, let no one separate." (NIV, Matthew 19:4-6).

This clearly states that God doesn't want us to divorce and the Church reinforces this message that marriage is sacred and divorce unacceptable. Some teachings may go as far as saying that divorcing is sinful and unforgivable. It is these teachings that have led to Christians staying in abusive marriages rather than getting divorced. Sadly, the fear of leaving a marriage and the fear of being condemned for doing so, has resulted in marriage partners being hurt, hospitalised or even killed.

While divorce is not part of God's plan for us, when studying the Bible further, it is clear that domestic violence is also in opposition to God's plan for families. As discussed, Genesis 1 depicts marriage as a one-flesh relationship in which each completes the other and they help each other without power and control. Nowhere in the Bible does it support a marriage that is built on power and control. Instead, we are given instructions to build relationships based on love:

"Love is patient and kind; love does not envy or boast; it is not arrogant or rude. It does not insist on its own way; it is not irritable or resentful; it does not rejoice at wrongdoing, but rejoices with the truth. Love bears all things,

believes all things, hopes all things, endures all things." (NIV, 1 Corinthians 13:4-7)

An abusive relationship isn't built on these things. It is built on lies, anger, hurt and dominance. An abusive relationship is, therefore, not built on love and is not part of God's plan for our relationships.

If the abuser is a Christian, he should be serving others, not manipulating and controlling them:

"Not so with you. Instead, whoever wants to become great among you must be your servant, and whoever wants to be first must be your slave — just as the Son of Man did not come to be served, but to serve, and to give his life as a ransom for many." (NIV Mathew 20:26-28)

Abusive controlling relationships are the very opposite of the Christian relationship that God desires us to have.

Repeatedly the Bible speaks out against violence and abuse. For example:

"The Lord examines the righteous, but the wicked, those who love violence, he hates with a passion." (NIV, Psalm 11:5)

It is not only physical violence that is condemned - verbal abuse is also criticised:

"Blessings crown the head of the righteous, but violence overwhelms the mouth of the wicked." (NIV, Proverbs 10:6)

And the Bible says that our choice of words that we use to others can cause damage or be used positively:

"The tongue has the power of life and death, and those who love it will eat its fruit." (NIV, Proverbs 18:21)

It is clear throughout the Bible that hurting others is not acceptable and not to be condoned in any form.

The Bible also recognises that there will be people in the world who are determined to hurt others through their own selfish needs. The description of these people sounds very much like those with Narcissistic Personality Disorder and the Bible clearly says that we should not go near them or have relationships with them:

"But mark this: There will be terrible times in the last days. People will be lovers of themselves, lovers of money, boastful, proud, abusive, disobedient to their parents, ungrateful, unholy, without love, unforgiving, slanderous, without self-control, brutal, not lovers of the good, treacherous, rash, conceited, lovers of pleasure rather than lovers of God — having a form of godliness but denying its power. Have nothing to do with such people." (NIV, 2 Timothy 3:1-7)

In contrast to hurting others for our own selfish needs, we are reminded that we should treat others with compassion and love in our relationships:

"Finally, all of you, be like-minded, be sympathetic, love one another, be compassionate and humble." (NIV, 1 Peter 3:8)

Rather than wanting people to hurt each other, God wants us to love each other. If He asks us to love our neighbours and our enemies, how can it then be acceptable for someone to hurt his partner when he should have the most loving relationship? It is clearly unacceptable for any partner to hurt the one he proclaims to love. God sets out what love is and hurting each other is not listed. The closeness of marriage, the coming together of two flesh into one flesh in a relationship is based only on love and not hurt.

The relationship based on love that God desires for us is evident in Ephesians:

"In this same way, husbands ought to love their wives as their own bodies. He who loves his wife loves himself. After all, no one ever hated their own body, but they feed and care for their body, just as Christ does the church— for we are members of his body. "For this reason a man will leave his father and mother and be united to his wife, and the two will become one flesh." This is a profound mystery — but I am talking about Christ and the church. However, each one of you also must love his wife as he loves himself, and the wife must respect her husband. (NIV, Ephesians 5:28-33)

The word 'love' is prevalent here and is the very foundation for our partnerships. Husbands should love their wives as much as themselves because they are as one, once they are joined together. Equally a wife should respect her husband in God's model of marriage.

An abusive relationship is not based on love and respect. It is based on power, control , fear and confusion. An abusive relationship is clearly not what God intended when He designed our partnerships. So, while God doesn't like marriage break ups, when they are not built on love and respect, they are not the relationship that He intended us to have.

God doesn't want us to be hurting and sent Jesus partly for the purpose of healing the brokenhearted and hurt, (which includes those who are or have been abused in their marriage) as he says here:

"The Spirit of the Lord is on me, because he has anointed me to proclaim good news to the poor. He has sent me to proclaim freedom for the prisoners and recovery of sight for the blind, to set the oppressed free, to proclaim the year of the Lord's favour." (NIV, Luke 4:18-19)

God doesn't want those suffering to continue to suffer. He wants us to be living the lives that He destined us to have, which isn't possible if we are living in fear, anxiety and confusion within an abusive relationship.

When there is abuse in a Christian relationship it is clear that God doesn't want that to continue, and neither does the partner who is being hurt. What often happens is that the she doesn't want to leave the marriage due to fearing condemnation from the Church if she does or that she will be seen as a sinner in the eyes of God. She also may feel pressure to forgive her partner as forgiveness is one of the central beliefs in the Christian Church and a command that Jesus gives us:

"So watch yourselves. "If your brother sins, rebuke him, and if he repents forgive him. If he sins against you seven times in a day, and seven times comes

back to you and says , 'I repent,' forgive him." (NIV, Luke 17 3-4)

We are told that we have to forgive no matter how many times someone sins against us. In an abusive Christian relationship, these verses of scripture may mean that someone stays in an abusive relationship, particularly if her partner continually says sorry for the hurt that he has caused. He may even say, "If you leave me then you haven't forgiven me and you're the sinner and the one in the wrong." This twists the responsibility back to his partner rather than him, which is a common trait of emotional abuse. It also demonstrates that there is an assumed link between forgiveness and staying in a relationship.

Forgiveness is not about the one who is hurting his partner through physical, verbal or emotional abuse, it is about the one being hurt and her relationship with God. God doesn't ask us to forgive and stay in that same situation to continue being abused. As explained, God doesn't want us to be in hurtful relationships but in loving relationships. Forgiveness isn't about continuing to be hurt but about letting go of negative feelings of anger, resentment and thoughts of revenge that will damage her further.

Forgiveness is also about giving a person, or situation, over to God for Him to deal with it, while seeking God's peace for hurt and direction for what to do within the relationship. It may well be that God desires marriage counselling or separation for her in order to protect her. Forgiveness doesn't mean that this is impossible.

Jesus not only commands us to forgive but also those who are sinning to repent. While a partner may say sorry to his partner, if he is truly repentant, the abusive behaviour will stop. If it continues, then arguably he is not repenting to the one that he has hurt. Repenting is not merely saying sorry. Anyone can say sorry and continue their actions. Repenting is also not providing a list of excuses for their behaviour, such as a difficult childhood, stress, alcohol, drugs , etc. Repenting for hurting others involves showing remorse, making amends, having a change of heart, changing behaviour from hurtful to loving and putting energy into rebuilding the relationship. If a partner is not willing to repent, then the other partner is not obligated to forgive him.

In addition, he needs to repent to God for God's forgiveness to occur and God to be able to change his heart so that he no longer hurts his partner. The relationship between God and the abuser is a private one and only God can know his heart. A partner may say that he has repented to God and He has been forgiven so his partner should too. However, the Bible commands that he should repent to both God and his partner who he has hurt. Suggesting that by repenting to God, nobody else has the right to judge his behaviour, or expect a change in behaviour, is not scripturally accurate.

When forgiveness happens, the hurting partner can let go of the emotions that may be causing further damage, such as anger and resentment. Forgiveness provides freedom for her and allows her to see the situation more clearly.

What forgiveness doesn't do is give him permission to continue to use power and control to hurt her further. Forgiveness also doesn't automatically mean reconciliation. She may forgive her partner but decide that she can no longer be in a relationship with him. The decision about the future of the relationship is one that she will have to consider carefully with prayer.

If she does decide that there can't be a reconciliation then she should feel able to end the relationship with a clear conscience. Marriage is a sacred union with vows and promises, but if one of the partners repeatedly breaks the vows and promises, hating rather than loving, he has broken that union and she is free to leave if she wishes.

Some may say that God hates divorce and quote Malachi 2:16 but God hates his children being abused more than divorce. We can see this because He sent His Son to heal the broken hearted and set free those being hurt:

"The Spirit of the Lord is on Me. He has put His hand on Me to preach the Good News to poor people. He has sent Me to heal those with a sad heart. He has sent Me to tell those who are being held that they can go free. He has sent Me to make the blind to see and to free those who are held because of

trouble. " (NIV, Luke 4:18)

Domestic abuse is in opposition to God's plan for marriage and it hurts the heart of God when families are destroyed by domestic abuse. However, God also heals those who have been hurt and offers freedom from abuse.

SECTION 7 – LOVING LIFE AGAIN

This section is for those who may have recognised that they are in an abusive relationship or want to help someone who they know is in an abusive relationship.

Recognising that you are in an abusive relationship is sometimes a shock. You may have realised that something is wrong for some time, but because your partner may not have hit you, or there was always a reason given for why he was behaving in that way, you may not have recognised it as abuse.

If you know that your relationship is abusive and that love is hurting you, you may be wondering what to do now.

Whatever you do, it is your choice. Nobody, including your partner, can say what is right for you or wrong for you. Many people may have opinions and voice them to you, but you have to decide what is best for you so that you are no longer hurting.

I ended my relationship after years of abusive behaviour that I didn't recognise for what it was. I am now no longer living in confusion, full of inner conflict, or feeling as though I am going mad. I am living a new life, which I am in control of, and I am loving it.

14
TO LEAVE OR STAY

I considered leaving at several points during my relationship with Mark, yet I stayed until the point that the police and social services were involved and effectively made the decision for me. There were many reasons that I stayed so long, and since the marriage ended many people have asked me why I didn't leave earlier. It is a complex matter and the passing of time has blurred my memories but these are some of the reasons that I remember for why I stayed:

- Wanting to keep my family together. I always saw myself having a husband and children and I always wanted a large happy family. When we had children, I wanted to give them the security of two parents and a stable home life. I believed that if there were problems in our marriage, that it was my responsibility to fix them for the sake of my family.

- Commitment to my marriage vows. As a Christian I took my marriage vows seriously, believed that marriage was for life and divorce was not an option. All marriages go through difficulties and I thought that, with some work, we could resolve them.

- Love for my husband. Despite all of his issues, and no matter how much he hurt me, I still loved him. It wasn't all negative and he could be a caring and thoughtful husband. I clung onto the hope that the loving side of Mark would be present all of the time and that our relationship would return to how it was when we first met. I only wanted the hurt to end but not to lose Mark completely.

- Fear for the future. Having been married from a young age I hadn't known adult life without Mark. I didn't know how or if I would manage bringing up a family by myself as I had never been alone. It is sometimes easier to stay in a bad situation than be in a new and unknown situation.

- Believing that things were normal. Being my only serious romantic relationship, it was hard to define what was normal and what wasn't as there wasn't much to compare it to. When I spoke to friends, they also felt hurt in their marriages at times and so I felt that it was just part of the ups and downs. It took talking to professionals to really open my eyes to what was happening.

- My Christian beliefs. As I discussed in the previous chapter, being a Christian can put additional pressure on you to stay in a negative relationship because of the beliefs regarding divorce and forgiving those who hurt us. At that time I interpreted the bible as saying that I couldn't leave without being sinful and forgiveness meant staying in the relationship.

- Believing that I could make him better. Mark explained his behaviour using his childhood, stress at work and his alcohol addiction. I thought that if he had counselling and I gave him support, he could overcome these issues and would then stop becoming angry and hurting me. I also believed that my marriage vows meant that I had to stay to help him as it was my duty to care for my husband.

- It's not that bad. As Mark had never hit me I thought it wasn't that bad. I thought, probably as many others do, that domestic abuse only involved hitting, punching or kicking. I didn't realise that just using his body to intimidate me was physical abuse. Nor did I realise that making me feel as though I was going crazy and manipulating me was emotional abuse. I stayed because I thought it wasn't as bad as other women's relationships as I wasn't being physically hurt.

You may recognise some of these reasons for staying in a relationship that is hurting you or has hurt you. There may also be other reasons for staying that will be unique to your relationship, but undoubtedly there will be a combination of factors. If there was one single reason, it would be easier to overcome but there are emotional and practical reasons why partners stay.

It will often take something extreme to happen before a partner will leave the relationship permanently. In fact, on average a woman will leave an abusive relationship seven times before she leaves for good.[16] Just as relationships are complex, leaving a relationship is complex.

The decision to leave is yours. An abusive partner won't want to be alone and won't suggest that your relationship ends. That places the decision onto you. The realisation that it is solely your decision whether to end your relationship or not may make you feel resentful or angry.

---

[16] www.domesticabuseshelter.org/infodomesticviolence.htm

15
LEAVING SAFELY

Leaving is often a process rather than an event. A process that may take years due to the cycle of someone abusing his partner, apologising, being caring and loving, then hurting her again.

If your relationship had no positives, it would be easier to leave, but abuse involves manipulation and using tactics to keep you in the relationship. For example, your partner changing to be the partner that you desire when it suits him.

Once the decision to leave has been made your safety needs to be the primary concern. It is well known that the most dangerous time for a woman in an abusive relationship is when she actually prepares to leave, when she leaves the home or just after she leaves.[17] This shouldn't deter you from leaving, but you need to have a plan to ensure that you (and your children) are safe.

Where to Live?

---

[17] www.domesticviolence.org

One of the first thoughts that is often prominent when thinking about leaving is where you will live. Leaving the family home can almost be as difficult as leaving the relationship because it is where memories were made, the children's bedrooms are, where time and money was spent getting the house to exactly how you wanted it. There were plans made when the house was bought and, by leaving, you may feel that the plans would be destroyed along with the dreams of having a safe happy home.

However, leaving a home can sometimes be the best option. As well as leaving the good memories, the bad memories will also be left behind. The time and money invested in the property was just that — putting energy into bricks and mortar — and while it can be very distressing to let that go, over time, it is possible to see it as somewhere that you lived in for a period of time, and now that period has finished.

I was fortunate enough to be able to stay in my home initially as it was Mark who left, but I was unable to stay there for long as I was the only one paying the joint mortgage which I couldn't afford so had to sell our home and move into rented accommodation. It was hard to say goodbye to the home that I loved and that I had decorated and changed. But, once I had left, I felt as though a weight had been lifted and I was feeling tentatively excited about having a fresh start. It is possible for you to have that fresh start too.

If you are staying in the home it will mean that your partner will have to leave and this may be difficult if he doesn't want the relationship to end. He could become aggressive and threatening if you try to force him out of the home so that you (and children, if you have any) can stay. Also, if he does leave, he could still see it as being his home and come back to try and persuade you to continue the relationship or to harass you.

If you do decide to stay in the home, and he is willing to move out, then it may be advisable for you to get an occupation order as this will prevent him being able to return to the home whenever he wishes to. An occupation order is issued by the court and a solicitor will usually be needed to help with the paperwork and to represent you in court. Ideally this process should be started as soon as he moves out for your own protection and security.

Sadly, leaving the home is often the easiest option, even if it feels that morally it should be the abusive partner that leaves.

As I've said safety needs to be the priority and for this reason sometimes a you might need to leave immediately. In an emergency situation you should always contact the police on 999.

If it is possible to plan beforehand, this will enable you to be able to sort out finances, housing, property and other aspects in advance, which should make the process less stressful.

If leaving the home, accommodation is important.

In an emergency and if you can't live in your own home because of domestic abuse your local council has a duty to give you housing information and to find you somewhere temporary to live. Temporary accommodation provided by the council will usually involve being placed in a hostel or bed and breakfast.

It may be that you are able to stay with your parents, other family or friends initially. However, if you can't stay with anyone or you choose not to, then finding a rental property initially is often the simplest option, rather than trying to purchase, which takes time and will be more complex. It may be worth talking to the council's housing benefit department to find out if you would be entitled to any help with your rent if you did leave the family home. Knowing whether there will be any assistance or not can help you to decide how much you can afford to pay for your monthly rent before you start looking for accommodation.

Estate agencies will usually want to take up personal and/or work references as well as doing a credit check. These can take a bit of time — often a couple of weeks or more — which is worth bearing in mind as it won't be possible to move in immediately. However, it is possible to start looking for a rental property and start the process while still living with a partner (and you won't need to tell him about it) so that it is complete and ready to move into on the day that you leave.

An estate agent will also typically want a deposit and a month's rent in advance. If you have savings to use for this and can manage to pay this without your partner's knowledge, then this is probably the simplest solution. If you don't have the funds (or your finances are in a joint account so that you can't access them without your partner finding out), you may have to borrow the money from close friends and family. Think carefully about who you tell about your plans to move out if you don't want your partner to find out. Another option is to use a rent deposit scheme which are usually run by local councils, housing associations or sometimes by a charity. It may also be worth speaking to the domestic abuse unit attached to the local police force if they have been involved.

Moving to a refuge is another possibility and any woman who has experienced any type of abuse can go to a refuge. You may stay for just a few days while alternative accommodation is being found, or you may stay for a few months for support. The charity 'Refuge' helps thousands of women every year and they have a free phone National Domestic Violence Helpline - 0808 2000 247 - to help women find spaces in refuges. The police and social services can also put women in touch with Refuge and other charities who can help with a place to stay.

What to Take?

Planning to leave while your partner is not home is the best option to avoid a potential confrontation.

Taking essential items is vital as it may not be possible to return to get them at a later date. Essentials such as:

- birth certificates
- passports
- identification
- financial information (such as bank statements)
- cheque books, debit cards and credit cards
- driving licence

- insurance documents
- mortgage or rental documents
- medication
- keys
- sentimental belongings (such as photographs)
- address book
- mobile phone and charger
- legal documents (such as court orders)
- bills that are in your name or joint names
- paperwork for debts that are in your name or joint names
- ownership documents for items or belongings that you own
- medical information
- child benefit/tax credit letters
- marriage certificate
- vehicle documents
- clothing
- toiletries
- children's favourite toys

It may be possible to take larger items such as furniture or electrical appliances. To do this a large van will probably be necessary, so this will need organising in advance.

Staying Safe after Leaving

After the end of the relationship, it is important to stay safe and protect yourself.

If you don't want your ex-partner to know where you are living, you can opt out of the open electoral register or register anonymously.

An ex-directory phone number will stop him being able to phone the house and dialling 141 before phoning your ex-partner will prevent him from being able to see your phone number.

If you have children you should tell their school, nursery or childminder what has happened, and let them know who will pick them up. You should also make sure they do not release the children to anyone else, or give your new address or telephone number to anyone.

Depending on where you work, and whether you feel your partner will try to contact you in the workplace, it may be advisable for you to tell your employer about the situation so that they are aware and don't pass out any information or let him into the building.

It is also advisable to change the passwords on your internet security — for example email accounts, social media accounts etc — as it is possible that he knows your passwords and will be able to see what you are doing online and potentially where you are.

If you have friends on social media who are also friends with your partner, you should consider whether to remain friends with them on social media because posting information on social media could be passed back to your ex-partner.

When in the house you should keep the doors and windows locked and not answer the door unless you are certain you know who is on the other side.

Depending on the age of your children you might wish to explain what has happened and why, as well as telling them not to give their father their new address or phone number.

Also, you should ensure that any paperwork that your ex-partner receives relating to you, such as court papers, doesn't have your address on it.

If you have any regular appointments that your ex-partner knows about (for example doctor's appointments), you should try to change the appointment time or the location of the appointment.

If your ex-partner continues to harasses, threaten or abuse you directly or indirectly (through others), it is important that you record every incident. If he is contacting you through emails, social media or text messages you should keep a copy of them or a screen shot as evidence. It is possible to get a non-molestation order if you are being harassed and the police may be able to support you to get this order in place. Alternatively, a solicitor will be able to help and you may be able to receive legal aid if there is evidence that there has been domestic abuse in the relationship.

16
FINANCES

You may have identified as yourself being emotionally abused in the Using Your Emotions chapter, and you may have little or no personal funds as a result of your partner taking control of the money in the relationship or running up debts. You may be worried about the financial impact of leaving the relationship if you have no money, are in debt or aren't working. You may be concerned about the long-term future alone without the financial support of your partner, even if he is being financially abusive, as he may be the one paying the mortgage or the bills.

However, there is financial help available and there is always a financial solution.

Before Leaving the Relationship

If you are planning to leave, the first thing that you may wish to consider doing is putting money aside for when you do. If your partner doesn't allow you access to money just try and put aside the odd pound or two from the change from the shopping; small amounts of money are less likely to be missed by your partner. Over time, small amounts can add up, but only try to do this if you can do so safely without your partner finding out.

If you don't have your own bank account, it is a good idea to set one up before you leave as benefits such as child benefit, housing benefit and tax credits can then be paid quickly into your account after you leave and you won't have to wait as long to start receiving payments. If you do set up an account before you leave, you may wish to request that paper copies of statements are not sent out so that your partner is unaware of your new account. Banks and building societies are encouraging more of us to go paper free and use internet banking, so this shouldn't be a problem. However, don't access the online banking from your home internet as your partner may be able to search your internet browsing history and find out. It is safer to use a friend's computer, your computer at work or go to the library.

As I've said in the previous chapter, if you can visit your local council's housing department before leaving and discuss options such as council property or housing benefit, then it will help you to be able to make plans. You may also be able to get help with the deposit and upfront rent for a property through the council, a housing association or charity.

If you've decided to stay in the family home you may be able to get some help with the mortgage interest payments through the Department of Work and Pensions. If you rent, you may be able to get housing benefit as the income into the house will be less without your partner, so it is worth contacting the local council to find out if you are eligible.

You may also wish to apply for an Occupation Order that states who is legally able to live in the home. A solicitor will be able to help with this. If you are concerned that you can't afford a solicitor, you may entitled to legal aid if there is evidence of domestic abuse and you are on a low income. A lot of solicitors will give half an hour of legal advice for free so it is worth finding out if your local solicitor will do this and speak to them regarding your edibility for legal aid and the possibility of getting an occupation order.

If you are wanting to take the mortgage over from your partner, and put it in just your name, you will need to speak to your bank or building society to see if they will lend you the mortgage amount that you need. If they won't lend you the mortgage and you have children, you can still stay in the property as long as you can afford the mortgage payments, as a judge will usually rule that a mother can stay in the family home until the children are 18 years of age.

However, it is worth bearing in mind that if the mortgage is in joint names, it is an asset that your partner owns and could possibly be used if your partner has debt that needs recovering.

Personally, knowing that Mark had thousands of pounds of debt and no job was a concern as I felt that he may go bankrupt and then there was a high possibility of losing the house while it was in joint names. In addition, having the house in joint names meant that we were financially connected on credit checks, so his debts would affect my credit rating for as long as we had a joint mortgage.

I applied for a mortgage in my own name, but despite my best efforts at working all the hours that I could, they couldn't give me the mortgage that I required to put the house in just my name. I was just £25,000 short. I remember that I cried at the building society when they told me and felt utter despair at not knowing what I was going to do or where I would live.

I finally decided to sell the house, although it felt awful. After paying a mortgage for 17 years it felt such a waste that I didn't have my own home at the end of it and would need to go back to renting. Selling our family home was very hard at the time, but I felt that had no choice. Looking back, it was for the best.

I now have a lovely house that I rent. I don't have to worry about anything going wrong in the house as I know that the agents will get it repaired at no cost to myself. I have no financial connection with my ex-husband so I'm financially free of him and his debts. It was so hard when I sold my house two years ago, but the weight has been lifted off my shoulders and I have no regrets.

It may be that your situation is different to mine and you don't have to move out or sell your home, but if you do it doesn't have to be a negative consequence of the end of a relationship - it can often be a fresh, new start.

After Leaving the Relationship

Once you have left you will need to get your finances sorted as soon as you can so that you don't have the stress of not knowing what is coming in or out and also to ensure that you are receiving the help that you need at this difficult time.

Firstly, it is always a good idea to do a budget so that you know if there is a shortfall or not. There are a lot of helpful budgeting sheets that you can fill out online or you could use a spreadsheet or even a notebook and pen. The important thing is to make sure that you know what money you have coming in and what your monthly bills, your weekly outgoings (such as a weekly food shop) and daily expenses (such as bus fares and dinner money) are.

Looking at old bank statements may give you an idea of some of the places that you are spending money and how much some of your outgoings may be. Although if you have moved into a new house you may not know how much some of the bills are yet, such as gas and electric. If this is the case you can go online to estimate your bills taking into account the size of your house and how many occupants there are living there. Council tax and water rates should also be online to give you an idea.

You may not have been on benefits previously but there is no shame in claiming benefits to help you through this period if you are finding yourself struggling and on a single income. When my marriage ended I lost Mark's income and, as the only one paying the mortgage and bills, I found myself financially struggling. Moving into a rented property meant that I received more help with paying for my home as I was able to claim housing benefit, which made a big difference. You may not want to claim benefits if you haven't done so previously, but they are there to help people who genuinely need them and, if you can't manage on one income and needed to leave an abusive partner, then you need them.

Whether you have children or not, if you work and are on a low income, you may be able to claim Working Tax Credit. You need to be working a minimum of 16 hours to be able to claim and whether you are entitled to it and how much you could receive is dependent on other factors, such as who else lives with you, whether someone in the household is disabled, your income etc.

If you have children you should already be receiving Child Benefit. If you have moved it is important to tell them of your new address as soon as possible. If you have changed your bank account, tell them of your new bank account as well. In addition to Child Benefit you may be able to receive Child Tax Credit which can supplement your wages and/or help you with your childcare. Again, whether you are entitled to it and how much you could receive is dependent on other factors.

To claim for either or both tax credits you will need to complete a claim form that you can order by either going online or by phoning the Tax Credits Helpline.

If you were claiming tax credits with your partner it is very important to contact the Tax Credits Helpline as soon as possible to tell them of your change in circumstances; i.e. being single, less income, house move, bank details change etc. Not doing so can result in an overpayment that you will have to pay back at a later date. It is also quite likely that without the income of your partner, you will be entitled to an increase in payments, which will help you at this difficult time.

If you are not working you may be entitled to Income Support (if you have a small child) or Jobseekers Allowance. The rates of these are fixed and can be found online as they change yearly. To claim these you will have to visit your local Jobcentre.

Whether you are renting or paying a mortgage, you may also be able to get help with your council tax depending on your income and savings. Again, it is worth enquiring with your local council to see if you are entitled to this help.

To get an idea of what you may be entitled to based on your income and in your particular situation, it is worth having a look at www.entitledto.co.uk or www.turn2us.org.uk both of which have an online calculator so you can put in your details and find out if you are eligible for any assistance.

There is other help that you may be entitled to such as free school meals and free prescriptions, and these will depend on the other benefits that you receive.

Separation of Finances

As I have explained I decided to sell the house in order to separate Mark and I financially. As well as the mortgage we also had a joint bank account that my wages went into and the bills were paid out of. In addition, Mark had his own bank account that his wages went into.

When we split up I asked for his debit card for the joint account so that I knew he couldn't take any funds out of it. As only my wages were paid into it and not Mark's I felt that he shouldn't have any access to it. Fortunately, Mark was in a good mood when I asked and he gave me his debit card. Unfortunately, just weeks later, he got into the house, took his debit card back and withdrew £600. As it was a joint account there was nothing that I, or anybody else could do, despite the fact that it was my money in the account and not his. A joint account means that anyone named on the account has full access to it and both partners can withdraw from the account without the other's permission.

As a result of my personal experience I would suggest visiting your bank and speaking to them in person at the first opportunity. It may be that they are able to freeze or close the account while it is being disputed, or offer alternative ways to help.

Joint debts are another issue that needs to be addressed as soon as possible. Our joint account was constantly overdrawn by £3,000. As it was in joint names we were jointly liable. I always believed that this meant we were liable for 50% each. Unfortunately, I found out that it meant we were liable for 100% each. This is the case for any joint debt.

As Mark had disappeared and was not staying at a permanent traceable address it meant that if a creditor wanted payment I would be the one who would be pursued for the debt. It seems unfair (and I said this a lot at the time) but it is the law. This is why it is important to try and know what debts there are and consider the possible solutions.

As I wanted to close the joint bank account, and sever that tie to him, I had to pay off the overdraft. While I could have asked him to pay it off, he wasn't working and had no means of paying it off. I also didn't want to ask him and open up contact. So, I borrowed £3,000 from family members in order to pay off the overdraft and to be able to close the account. It meant that I had to pay 100% of a joint debt, which seems unfair, but it was a means to an end and that was to remove Mark from my life, which was more important to me than £3,000.

Paying the debt off is only one solution and there are many others depending on your situation and circumstances. There are places to turn if you need help with debt - such as the Citizens Advice Bureau, Step Change and Christians Against Poverty - all of whom are able to offer impartial advice.

If you don't know if you are financially linked, or if your name is tied to any debts, it is worth requesting a credit check which will show up any financial associations and debts. Experian will do it for free in the first 30 days but you need to remember to cancel your membership before the end of this time if you don't want to be paying a monthly fee.

Having joint debts may be a concern when leaving a relationship but it shouldn't be a reason to stay. Your mental, physical and emotional health are more important than debts. There are solutions for debts and any other money issues that can arise.

Child Maintenance

If you have children together then your partner has a responsibility to contribute towards their upbringing. This is not dependent on whether or not he sees his children. Access to children and contributing financially are two separate issues.

If there has been abuse, keeping contact with your ex-partner to nothing or as little as possible is best, so you may need to apply to the Child Maintenance Service (CMS) to receive financial support. If you do wish to work it out between yourselves and are trying to calculate how much he should be paying, there is a useful calculator on the Government website to assist you.

To use the Child Maintenance Service there is a £20 application fee. However, you don't have to pay the application fee if you have experienced domestic abuse or you're under 18.

Once you have applied, the CMS will check your partner's income with Her Majesty's Revenue & Customs (HMRC), calculate how much he should be paying and create a schedule for the payments.

If your ex-partner agrees and pays the money directly to you, then the CMS don't do anything further. However, there are charges if the Child Maintenance Service has to step in to collect money from your ex-partner and pay it to you. This currently costs the parent who is claiming for the child maintenance 4% of the amount collected. So, if they are awarded £10 a week, they would actually receive £9.60 of it with the CMS keeping the 4% fee. The paying parent has to pay an additional 20% on top of the usual child maintenance amount.

Being Free

If you were in a financially abusive relationship that involved you not having control of the money, being free of your partner also means having freedom with your money. It means that you can spend it on what you would like to and there won't be consequences. It may also mean that you won't have debts that are out of your control. Your finances will be in your power.

For the first time in my adult life I am not living in an overdraft and I know that I'm not in debt or married to someone who is. It feels amazing.

17
HEALING THE HURT

Leaving an abusive relationship can be one of the hardest things someone does and even after your ex-partner is out of your life, sometimes the emotional and mental affects from experiencing abuse can linger on as explained in the Effects on the Partner chapter.

However, it is also possible to not only leave an abusive relationship, but to rebuild yourself so that you are stronger, more confident and free to love life again.

Whether you have chosen to stay in the relationship (if he has changed) or leave your partner, healing your hurt is vital to being happy again. What is important to note is that there is no one way to feel or heal after you leave an abusive relationship.

You are Worthy

You have taken the first step by recognising that you are or were in an abusive relationship. You now need to believe that you were in no part responsible for his actions and didn't deserve any of his actions or his treatment of you. It was nothing that you did or didn't do. There was nothing that you could have done differently that would have changed his behaviour. He chose to behave in that way. He chose to hurt you. Not because of the person that you are or what you did or didn't do, but because he enjoys control and power.

The corrosive effect of living in an abusive relationship is destroyed self-esteem. Being put down, undermined, manipulated and disrespected can result in believing that you are unworthy of being treated well or don't deserve anything good to happen in your life.

Changing your thought patterns from worthlessness to being worthy of being happy can take a while and may be hard, but it is possible. Once you believe that you are worthy of happiness, your partner loses his hold on you. His control and power come through making you believe that you are nothing without him and don't deserve happiness. So the first thing is to believe that you are worth being treated well and deserve to be happy instead of being hurt.

Setting boundaries is important to your belief that you are of value. Healthy boundaries define who we are in relation to those around us by helping us to know the limits that we are willing to go to are with others. Personal boundaries are how we teach people who we are and how we would like to be handled in relationships. Whether you have decided to stay in the relationship or leave, boundaries are vital to respecting yourself and expecting others to respect your thoughts and feelings. People with healthy self-esteem have strong personal boundaries and practising strong personal boundaries builds self-esteem. Boundaries and self-esteem are intrinsically linked. By setting boundaries, you are not being selfish or unloving towards others, you are accepting yourself, which leads to forming healthy relationships with those who will respect you, not hurt you.

Learning to set boundaries can be difficult if you have not done it in your relationships before. You may not be used to saying no to people, and even feel guilty for doing so, but saying no establishes that you have self-respect and aren't willing to be dominated or manipulated. If something makes you feel uncomfortable, resentful or hurt, then it is important for your own well-being to be able to say no to it.

It may take a while to get used to saying no and it may also take a while for those around you to get used to you setting boundaries. But by continuing to reinforce them, you will find that they will get used to them over time and adjust their view of you. You may even find that you attract new people into your life who are supportive and like-minded.

If someone doesn't take any notice when you have said no, then you may need to explain what they are doing or walk away if it is making you feel negative.

On the other hand, it is positive to let those who do respect your boundaries know what a beneficial impact it is having on your life. This will help to build up healthy relationships.

Trust your instincts and inner voice about what you do and who you want in your life. By trusting yourself and believing that you can make the right decisions, you will find that your confidence in yourself will grow and fear will reduce. Establishing boundaries will show others that you respect yourself and expect to be treated with respect.

Grieving

When a relationship ends there is often a period of grieving, even if you chose to end the relationship. It's perfectly normal to feel sad, lost or angry after a relationship breaks down. These feelings are also normal if you were in an abusive relationship. Even though there may have been some very difficult times, and you were hurting physically and/or emotionally, there were still happy moments in the relationship.

This mixture of positive and painful memories may leave you feeling confused about the range of emotions that they produce. You may even feel that you shouldn't be grieving the relationship because of the abuse that you suffered. On the other hand, you may feel guilty for not being as sad as you feel you should be when you think about the positive memories. You may also be doubting some of your memories and wondering if it was better or worse than you recall.

Everyone will feel differently about the memories of their relationship but most will feel a mixture of emotions which don't always make sense. This is also part of the fog of confusion that you are taking with you from being in an abusive relationship. Living with a relationship that cycles through happy periods, tension building and then explosions results in doubting your own emotions and not being able to trust others or yourself. Even after the end of the relationship this fog of confusion can remain, and you may be unsure how you feel.

Accepting that you feel a range of emotions, and that is normal and healthy, is part of being able to move on. However you feel about your partner, the past and the present, is right for you at the time.

Emotions change over time and you may find yourself shifting through a range of emotions as you grieve the end of a period of your life. Just like mourning the death of someone, you may find that you move through stages such as denial, guilt, anger, reflection, depression, acceptance and hope. There is no right way or wrong way to grieve. Some may go through all the stages, others may go through only some of the stages and some may do them in a different order.

Remember that it is not just a relationship that you are grieving for; it is also the hopes and dreams that you had for that relationship. The dream of finding the person who would treat you well, understand you and support you. You may have believed that the person was your soul mate, especially at the start of the relationship when he appeared to idolise you and made you feel special. Trying to hold onto the thought that he is that person you fell in love with, and who loves you, is what kept you in the relationship until this point. Now that you have recognised that the relationship was abusive, it is time to grieve for what you may have thought it was and what you thought it may have evolved into. The feelings of loss of what could have been and what you thought it was can be profound.

Personally, I know that I grieved my dream of a large, happy family far more than I grieved the reality. As I always hoped that there would be a happy ending and that Mark could get better, realising that this was never going to happen felt as though I had lost something that I had clung to. I also felt sadness at losing the person that I thought Mark was — the person who I had fallen in love with and who re-emerged at times. I don't know how much of that Mark was real and how much was false, but to me, at the time, he was real and despite everything that had happened I had to keep the hope that he was coming back. By accepting that the loving 'Mark' and my dream of a two parent family unit had died meant I could grieve and move on.

Your loss and grief deserve your acceptance and tenderness. Take your time.

Self-blame

Part of being in an abusive relationship is feeling that everything is down to you. He refused to take any responsibility for his actions and passed the blame onto a range of alternatives. You probably felt as though you were the one responsible for healing him and making him better. You probably tried a wide range of tactics to try and help him. But you also found that nothing worked or it only worked for a short period of time.

Taking on the responsibility of the hurt in the relationship is part of the manipulation techniques that he used. Even after the relationship ends, you may still feel in some way responsible and blame yourself for his actions. You may be wondering if, had you done something differently, he wouldn't have reacted in the way that he had. You may wonder whether if you had helped him a little more or for a bit longer, he would have got better and returned to the person you knew at the start of the relationship. These feeling are typical if you have been in an abusive relationship.

After you have come to the realisation that you weren't to blame for his actions, that they were his choice and there was nothing that you could have done to have changed that, you may feel a different type of self-blame. You may blame yourself for not recognising what was happening and ending the relationship earlier. You may look back at times when you did think his actions were abusive and feel guilt that you didn't listen to your intuition and leave. However, the truth is that every time you saw it, he manipulated you with his lies and false promises, creating a fog of confusion and ensuring that you doubted yourself.

At the time, you didn't know that you were being manipulated — that is how manipulation works. It is often some time later when you are free of the relationship and the lies that you start to be able to see the truth and move the blame from your shoulders to the person who was responsible — your ex-partner.

Once you are able to do that your emotional health will improve. You will no longer be holding onto the guilt and shame that blaming yourself results in. You will feel free of these emotions and be able to feel worthy of being happy.

Anger

During the relationship there were probably many times when you felt angry at something your partner said or did. Times at which you felt you were being unjustly accused of something, were lied to, given the silent treatment or hurt through words or actions. It is also likely that when you expressed your anger your partner turned it around to make it appear as though you were the one that was being unreasonable in the relationship and causing problems through your emotional outburst. I certainly know that is what happened in my relationship. Mark would accuse me of having issues with my temper if I shouted back at him and would accuse me of being out of control and unsafe.

Over time your frustration at not being able to express your emotions at his treatment of you, or his responses to your emotions, may have led to feeling as though you were going crazy. Suppressed anger and frustration grows rather than diminishes.

It is no wonder then, that when you leave the relationship, you may feel very angry at the person who has made you feel this way, as well as anger at his treatment of you. Rather than continuing to suppress your anger, it is important that it is let out for your mental and emotional well-being.

Expressing your frustrations and anger in a safe way is important. Here are some suggestions for releasing these emotions but you may find others that work for you.

- Hug a pillow as tight as you can or scream into your pillow.

- Write a letter to your ex-partner to tell him why you are angry at him then burn it when you have finished it.

- Do some physical exercise like running, dancing, swimming or cycling.

- Use a breathing technique. For example, imagine that you are sat on a beach on a warm, sunny day with nobody else there. Breathe in through your nose and watch a wave gently lapping the shore. Breathe out through your mouth slowly and blow the wave out to the horizon as far as you can see. In addition, you can put a word on the wave that sums up why you are angry and blow it out until you can no longer see it.

- Express yourself in art — painting or drawing. It doesn't need to look like anything, just pick some colours and let yourself loose.

- Talk to someone. Ring a close friend or pop around to see them and have a rant about what it is that is making you feel angry.

- Go for a walk and kick leaves, stamp in the mud or enjoy the nature.

- Listen to angry music and sing/shout along to it.

If the anger is affecting you and your family then you may need to talk to a professional to be able to express your emotions about the relationship.

Forgiving

With all the hurt that your ex-partner has caused you to feel, as well as practical problems (such as finances and housing), it is understandable that you may resent your ex-partner for what he has done or what he is doing. I know there were many times that I resented the fact that Mark had just walked away leaving me with a big mess to sort out. Most of the time the logical part of me won over and I knew that life was better without him. But there were days when I was consumed with resentment because I was exhausted from being up most of the night with a small baby, working several jobs because I was the only one paying the mortgage, dealing with toddlers and teenagers, as well as trying to deal with legal paperwork and financial affairs while my ex-partner had no responsibilities.

What did the resentment achieve? Nothing. It didn't make me sleep better. It didn't help with looking after the house or the children. It didn't complete the piles of forms or make the necessary phone calls to sort things out. All it did was make me feel worse. It made me feel more like a victim and that he had won. Resentment sapped me of energy and made me look at my life negatively. I couldn't see how I was blessed or anything positive about my situation.

Choosing to forgive, letting go of the resentment and looking for the positive, changes how you look at everything else in your life. By focusing your emotions on the person that hurt you, you stay chained to them. You stay chained to them because you resent that they are doing things that you are not. You resent that they have left you with problems and have got away with it. You resent what they have taken away and yet they seem to have it all. Through this resentment it can seem as though they have won and you have lost which can make you feel like a victim. And victims are powerless.

To take back the power and control you have to let go of the resentment that is pulling your thoughts and emotions back to him. The only way to do that is to let go.

Many feel that by forgiving it would let their ex-partner off the hook or mean that they are condoning his behaviour. Forgiveness is not about forgetting, trusting him again or saying that his behaviour was acceptable. It is also not a sign of weakness, being a fool or having a duty to forgive.

Forgiveness is not allowing the hurt to eat you up, not seeing yourself as the victim and not living with negative emotions that ruin your other relationships. Forgiveness is about taking back control of your life, trusting your own instincts, finding self-acceptance, creating boundaries and seeing the positives.

Forgiveness doesn't help the person that hurt you. Forgiveness helps you.

Your ex-partner doesn't need to know that you have forgiven him for you to benefit. It is something that is private and that you can do without telling anyone.

If you still feel as though there is a fog of confusion around your relationship and the events, a suggestion is to write down every situation in which you felt hurt. It may take a while and you may think of more once you start writing, but write down every memory of hurt. Don't worry if this takes weeks to do or you can only do a little each day – it is more important to get it all out than rush it.

Once you've done this, read each one through and say, "I forgive you. I am ready to let go. I am happy now." You may not feel as though you mean it, but each time that you do this you loosen up the chains that bind you and implant positive messages on your mind. Re-read the list and say, "I forgive you. I am ready to let go. I am happy now," as many times as you need to over days, weeks or months.

Professional Support

You may feel as though you would like additional help to deal with the mixture and strength of your emotions. Talking to another person can be very beneficial for you to be able to work through that fog and help you to see the issues more clearly. Sometimes a friend is able to support you through this time, but sometimes it may need someone with more experience and knowledge of domestic abuse.

There are NHS and private counsellors, cognitive behavioural therapists and hypnotherapists who can help you to sort through your thoughts and feelings and help you feel more positive and in control. Speaking to your doctor about how you feel would be a good place to start and will enable you to understand what options for help there are.

You may also benefit from medication to help if you are feeling low or anxious. Again, your doctor will be the best person to speak to. Asking for and accepting help can be difficult but it is also a sign that you wish to move on and get better.

18
LOVING LIFE

If you feel as though you have started to heal and let go of the past and its chains, then it is time to start loving life again.

Freedom

Being by yourself may feel strange if you have been in a long-term relationship but it can also be a fantastic time. For the first time in a long time, you have space to breathe and focus on yourself.

When you were with your ex-partner you may have felt restricted by what you could or couldn't do due to his expectations, consequences or financial constraints.

However, now is your time. You are free to make your own decisions, to take control of your life and embrace every moment. You are no longer tied to someone who couldn't be reasoned with. You are free to have the life that you deserve.

Your Appearance

Since I have let go of my past I have changed things in my life. One thing is my appearance. I have taken a lot of my old clothes to charity shops and bought new clothes and shoes that I never thought I would wear. I have been to a salon for the first time in my life and had massages, manicures, my nails painted and a facial or two. After over a decade with the same haircut, I also decided to have a change and chop it off. Changing my appearance has been fun and increased my confidence. It has been a statement that I am ready to start my new life.

If you fancy the idea of changing your usual look, then why not? You don't have to please a partner, you can just please yourself. Try a new make up brand, a different style of clothes or dye your hair. Have fun and experiment.

Decorating

Whether you have stayed in your home or moved somewhere new, a change of colour in your environment can make you feel so different. Maybe you've always wanted a pink bedroom but your ex-partner wouldn't let you. Now, you can just go with whatever takes your fancy. Try a new colour on the walls, spruce up the woodwork or put up a new curtain and see how it makes you feel.

The great thing about decorating is that if you don't like it, you can change it. If you get bored, you can change it. Enjoy yourself and express your new life through paint and colour.

Hobbies

Have you ever wanted to try something new but not had the time, money or courage to do it? Why not try something new now?

After Mark and I split up, my mum encouraged me to try Ballroom and Latin dancing. I last had a Ballroom and Latin dance lesson when I was about 8 years old so was a little anxious about dancing again. However, I loved it and less than two years later, I have passed my Bronze, Silver and Gold medals.

My new hobby gives me space to do something just for me. For that hour a week I don't have to think about anything else and I just enjoy myself. It is my time of the week to refresh and replenish myself.

You don't have to start dancing (although you can if it takes your fancy); it might be that you've always wanted to paint, sew or write. Maybe you want to start an exercise class or take up a new sport. Whatever it is you now have the freedom to try it.

See if there is a class nearby that you would be interested in. Or try something new at home. Do something for you and enjoy treating yourself with a new hobby.

Work

If you felt unable to work due to your ex-partner, but wanted to, then you may want to consider looking for a job that interests you. Something that you will enjoy and will give you a sense of satisfaction.

Alternatively, if you are already working but not happy, then why not do something new? See what other positions there are in your current place of employment, look at other possible jobs or even consider starting your own business.

Think about what you would like to do in an ideal world and then see if you can do it. A dream job doesn't have to stay as a dream - it can become a reality.

If you need some extra qualifications to achieve your dream job ask at your local college or maybe try the Open University.

If you decide that your dream is to work for yourself there is also help out there and most of it is free. If you are on benefits you can speak to your benefit adviser to see if there are any courses or funding to help you. There are also grants and loans to help those wanting to start their own business. You can find lots of advice online and two places that you may want to start with are www.startups.co.uk and www.startupdonut.co.uk.

Fear

The most important thing is to take some time to listen to yourself and be clear about what you want to do. Don't let fear stop you from realising your dreams. Your fear may stem from other people's negative words - don't let them stop you. Instead, take a deep breath and go for it.

I admit that I'm feeling fearful as I write this book. I worry that nobody will read it and, if someone does, they will think it is awful. I worry about what others think about my words and about me. Yet, I am also learning to rise above those worries and fears and fulfil my dream of writing and helping others. Fears are there to be overcome so that you can grow as a person and be happy.

You have come this far and overcome so many challenges along the way that overcoming fear is more than achievable. Don't let fear stop you.

Trusting and Loving Again

When you have been betrayed, manipulated and lied to, it is difficult to trust again. Yet a life without trust means a life without close relationships. We need relationships to be happy. It doesn't mean we have to be in a romantic relationship, but being close to others in a range of relationships makes us feel more complete and happy.

Of course, with any relationship there is the risk of betrayal and being hurt. Yet, with isolation comes the risk of loneliness and unhappiness.

To trust again you need to feel confident in yourself and be able to trust in your own feelings.

You may feel that you were confident and secure before you met your ex-partner, yet he was still able to manipulate you, so how can you believe in your own intuition and feelings again? What you have to remember is that at the start of the relationship he was probably showing himself to be trustworthy and so you would have rightly trusted him. Later, when he started the manipulation, you continued to trust him because you had the perception that he was trustworthy at the start of the relationship.

You may be thinking that as it had happened before, that it may happen again in the same way. However, this time you are aware of the tactics that can be used to manipulate and betray you. You have an awareness that you didn't have before and you know that you need to listen to your feelings closely. If something doesn't feel right, you won't brush it off as you may have done in the past, but examine it more closely.

Believing in your own intuition and feelings comes from having confidence and belief in yourself. Once you trust yourself and your ability to be strong, you can trust in others.

A lot of people who have been in an abusive relationship have benefited from doing the Freedom Programme. It can be done online or in person and helps you to be able to see what was going on in your past relationships and recognise the early signs of abuse so that it won't be repeated in the future. It helps to change your perceptions and thinking to give you the freedom to trust again. I would highly recommend it and you can see further details on their website – see Further Help.

Remember

You are in charge of your new journey and your new life. Embrace this new adventure and love every step of it. The possibilities are endless.

NOTES FROM THE AUTHOR

I hope that you have found this book informative and helpful. Before I wrote this book, I had a blog in which I briefly described some of the elements of my marriage and why my marriage had ended. I explained that I felt it wasn't an abusive relationship until it was over and talked about my confusion that I had felt leading to the end of our relationship.

A few months after my blog post, I met a mum in a local play area and she asked what I did for a job so I told her that I write a blog. I thought nothing more of it until the next day when she emailed me and explained that she had read my blog and it resonated with her. She could see many similarities in the way that her boyfriend treated her and the way that my ex-husband treated me. She told me that she had phoned her mum and was going to move in with her as she couldn't mentally cope with her boyfriend's verbal and emotional abuse any longer. Like me, she hadn't recognised her relationship as being abusive until it had caused her pain.

When I decided to write this book, my intention was to help those who felt that they are hurting in their relationship but didn't know why. If this book helps just one person to see through the fog of confusion, break free and be happy again, then I will have achieved my intention.

As for me, how did my story end?

Well, two and a half years after my marriage ended and after deciding that being single was much better, someone showed me that it is possible to have a relationship based on love and respect rather than power and control. As I type this, I am also busy organising our wedding and by the time you are reading this, I will be married to a wonderful considerate man who makes me very happy.

ABOUT THE AUTHOR

J Davey is the author of *If Love Hurts* and has first-hand experience of living in an abusive relationship. She was in a relationship for nearly 20 years, during which her husband used his physical body, words and actions to control the relationship. After one particular episode, the police and social services became involved in her and her children's lives and she decided to end the marriage.

Writing her account of domestic abuse on her blog, she received many positive comments and some women contacted her directly asking for support. As a result, she wrote *If Love Hurts* to help other women who, like herself may have not realized that they were in an abusive relationship until it has done some damage.

J Davey also has a website and Facebook group to help anyone who feels that they may be in an abusive relationship or who want further resources:

www.iflovehurts.co.uk

www.facebook.com/groups/iflovehurts

FURTHER HELP

If you are experiencing domestic violence:
- Freephone 24 hour Domestic Violence Helpline. This service offers a 24 hour confidential helpline for women who are experiencing domestic violence with referral to refuges and other local support: 0808 2000 247
- Refuge's website has information for women experiencing domestic violence, including support on financial issues: www.refuge.org.uk

Legal advice:
- Community Legal Services Direct: www.clsdirect.org.uk or 0845 345 4345
- The Law Society (information about local solicitors): www.lawsociety.org.uk or 020 7242 1222
- National Centre for Domestic Violence: www.ncdv.org.uk or 0870 922 0704
- Rights of Women: www.rightsofwomen.org.uk

Advice on housing:
- Shelter: www.shelter.org.uk or 0808 800 4444

Information about benefits:
- Department for Work and Pensions: www.dwp.gov.uk
- Job Centre Plus: www.jobcentreplus.gov.uk
- Citizen's Advice Bureau: www.adviceguide.org.uk

Information about working tax and child credits:
- Her Majesty's Revenue and Customs: www.hmrc.gov.uk/taxcredits

Advice on child maintenance:
- Child Maintenance Enforcement Commission's Advice and Information Service www.dsdni.gov.uk/index/csa/cmed-iss.htm or 0800 028 7439

Credit check:
- Experian: www.experian.co.uk

Advice on financial issues:
- National Debtline: 0808 808 4000
- Christian Against Poverty: www.capek.org
- Money Made Clear: www.moneymadeclear.fsa.gov.uk

Help for getting over the abuse and living life again:
- http://iwmm.net/
- www.iflovehurts.co.uk
- www.freedomprogamme.co.uk

IF LOVE HURTS

60085295R00091

Made in the USA
Charleston, SC
19 August 2016